Methods of
FAMILY
RESEARCH

D0167583

For Rachel, J.J., and Sam

Methods of
FAMILY
RESEARCH

SECOND EDITION

Theodore N. Greenstein
North Carolina State University

SAGE Publications
Thousand Oaks ▪ London ▪ New Delhi

Copyright © 2006 by Sage Publications, Inc.

All rights reserved. No part of this book may be reproduced or utilized in any form or by any means, electronic or mechanical, including photocopying, recording, or by any information storage and retrieval system, without permission in writing from the publisher.

For information:

Sage Publications, Inc.
2455 Teller Road
Thousand Oaks, California 91320
E-mail: order@sagepub.com

Sage Publications Ltd.
1 Oliver's Yard
55 City Road
London EC1Y 1SP
United Kingdom

Sage Publications India Pvt. Ltd.
B-42, Panchsheel Enclave
Post Box 4109
New Delhi 110 017 India

Printed in the United States of America.

Library of Congress Cataloging-in-Publication Data

Greenstein, Theodore N.
Methods of family research / Theodore N. Greenstein.— 2nd ed.
    p. cm.
Includes bibliographical references and index.
ISBN 1-4129-1677-1 (pbk.)
    1. Family—Research—Methodology. 2. Social sciences—Research—Methodology. I. Title.
HQ10.G724 2006
306.85′072—dc22   2005023034

This book is printed on acid-free paper.

06 07 08 09 10 9 8 7 6 5 4 3 2 1

Acquiring Editors:	Jim Brace-Thompson and Cheri Dellelo
Editorial Assistant:	Karen Ehrmann
Project Editor:	Jenn Reese
Typesetter:	C&M Digitals (P) Ltd.

Brief Contents

Detailed Contents

Preface

I first taught research methods more than a quarter of a century ago. Each time I taught the course, I became increasingly convinced that the approach I was taking was all wrong. I was trying to teach people how to *do* research—to give them a metaphorical toolbox of technical skills so that they could someday design and conduct their own research. Although I knew that few of my students would actually do research, I continued to teach the course the same way.

When Sage asked me to write this text, I realized that I had an opportunity to correct this mistake. *Methods of Family Research* reflects my philosophy that what most people want (and need) to learn about family research methods is not how to *do* research on families but how to *read* research on families. Few of you will become active researchers, but all of you will need to know how to read and interpret research reports. Whether you work in a commercial organization, a government agency, or some not-for-profit group involved with families and children, you must be able to critically examine reports of research relevant to your work. Becoming a critical consumer of research reports is important even if you don't find employment in a family-related field, because our daily lives are increasingly filled with research findings. Newspapers, the Internet, television, and magazines routinely report results of opinion polls, evaluations of social programs, and other research. Without some understanding of research methods, it's impossible to be an active and knowledgeable twenty-first-century citizen. *Methods of Family Research* will help you to acquire this understanding.

The Goal of This Text

The goal of this text is *not* to teach you to be a researcher. No single book or course can do that. Instead, this text is aimed at helping you become an intelligent and critical *consumer* of research on families. To that end, the text will introduce you to how research on families is conducted and how to read journal articles and books reporting such research. The focus will be on interpreting and understanding research techniques commonly used in research on families rather than the mechanics of actually doing the research.

By the time that you finish this text, you should be competent to read and evaluate published reports of research on families. This is a valuable skill, because we are inundated with reports of research findings every day. Whether you plan to be a practitioner, a teacher, or an administrator, some knowledge of research methods will be essential to your career success. Some of you may even be inspired to seek out additional training so that you can become a producer of social research yourself.

What's New in the Second Edition

The structure of this new edition is similar to that of the first edition, with some important additions. Most notably, there is new coverage (Chapter 8) on mixed methods in family research. Chapter 7 on qualitative methods has been expanded and now includes a section on diary methods. New information about reliability and validity issues has been added to Chapter 5. Many new examples and study questions have been added throughout the text. The For Further Reading lists at the end of each chapter have been revised to take into account new publications since the release of the first edition. Input from colleagues and students using the text has been used to improve both the content and the style of the text, and hardly a page has not been revised or updated.

To the Student

This text has several features to aid in the learning process. Key terms and concepts are **boldface** when they first appear in the text; all the boldface terms appear and are defined in the Glossary. The Glossary also serves as an index, because the page number(s) on which each term is discussed appear there, as well. The For Further Reading lists at the end of each chapter present additional or more advanced treatments of the issues discussed in the text. Exercises designed to enhance your skills appear in the Study Questions sections. Even if your instructor doesn't require you to do these exercises, you may find that they help you to prepare for exams.

To the Instructor

I've never encountered a text that completely fulfills my needs in teaching a course, and *Methods of Family Research* is no exception. I expect that you will want to supplement the text with an assortment of journal articles and research monographs (and possibly newspaper and magazine articles) reporting relevant research. I have presented more examples in the text, all of which appear in the For Further Reading sections. If time permits, you may want to assign the original articles to your students.

You may wish to create a set of readings organized around research strategy: one article using sample survey methods, another using an experimental design, and so forth. Or you might assign different research monographs to a number of student teams for classroom critique. One valuable extended exercise is to find a newspaper or magazine article reporting some family-related study, then assign both that article and the original research report for reading and comparison by the students. Students will be amazed at the discrepancies between the actual research and how it is reported in the popular press! Throughout your course, I hope you will emphasize that simply because a piece of research is published—even if it's in a major journal—doesn't mean the study is perfect. On the contrary, encourage your students to critically analyze what they read.

Organization of This Text

In general, the sequencing of chapters in *Methods of Family Research* follows the usual flow of the research process. Chapter 1 begins by discussing the nature of research on families and some relevant issues in the philosophy of science. Chapter 2 presents the crucial concept *variable* and the various theoretical roles that variables can occupy in family research. Chapter 3 analyzes the structure of a typical research article in a professional journal and provides an introduction to literature searches. The Internet as a source of information and data for family research is the focus of Chapter 4. In Chapter 5, the key issues of measurement and operationalization are introduced. Chapters 6 and 7 outline the basics of quantitative and qualitative research strategies, whereas Chapter 8 introduces the idea of mixed methodologies. Chapter 9 provides an overview of sampling procedures. Creating and finding scales and indices is the topic of Chapter 10. Chapter 11 serves as a brief introduction to descriptive and inferential statistical techniques. Evaluating applied family programs is discussed in Chapter 12. Chapter 13 covers the increasingly important topic of using and locating secondary data sets. Finally, political and ethical issues in family research are presented in Chapter 14.

However, I encourage instructors to rearrange the chapters as they see fit. For example, some will want to cover ethical issues (Chapter 14) earlier in the course. Others may want to discuss scales and indices (Chapter 10) immediately after measurement (Chapter 5). You may prefer to cover sampling (Chapter 9) before discussing data collection strategies (Chapters 6, 7, and 8).

Acknowledgments

I owe a great debt to the instructors who introduced me to social research methods. Bill Crano sparked my interest in social research when I was an undergraduate at Michigan State University. Michael Allen, Duane Alwin, Howard Bahr, Charlie Bowerman, Lew Carter, Lee Freese, Vik Gecas, Gary Lee, and especially Louis Gray shaped my thinking about methods as a graduate student at Washington State University.

My colleagues at North Carolina State University—especially Ron Czaja and Cathy Zimmer—read various sections of this text. NC State also provided a research leave to work on the first draft of the manuscript during its early stages. Sage Series Editors Dave Klein of Notre Dame and Bert Adams of Wisconsin made extensive comments and suggestions throughout the writing process. I would also like to thank the following reviewers who provided valuable suggestions for the Second Edition: Barbara D. Ames; Charles A. Calahan; Adam Davey; Kory Floyd; Sandra L. Hofferth; Carol Markstrom, Ph.D.; Mary Ann Powell, Ph.D.; Frankie Rabon; Amanda Duffy Randall; and Hiromi Taniguchi; as well as the many anonymous individuals who were so generous with their feedback. Any errors, of course, are my own.

1

Why Do Research on Families?

To many people, *doing research* on families seems a waste of time. After all, we all have families, don't we? We know about families through our own experiences. Most surveys simply confirm what we already know, right? So why bother to do social research on families?

To really understand why we do social research, we have to recognize that curiosity is one of the most basic of human drives. Some biologists believe that the human brain is hardwired to solve challenges and answer questions. It's probably this drive that led the human species from learning to light fires to landing on the moon within a few hundred generations. Humans seem to have an innate need to know why things happen the way they do. Albert Einstein reportedly said, "God does not play dice with the universe," meaning that we don't like to believe that events simply happen. We need or want to believe that events happen for reasons. Much human activity is centered on discovering these reasons, a major manifestation of which is the search for personal understanding—the need to know why things happen.

When we find ourselves in an ambiguous or unfamiliar setting, we often feel a need to impose some kind of structure to help us make sense of it. Answering the *why* question helps to impose that structure. We have an innate need to understand: why family sizes are declining; why some husbands abuse their wives; why children from certain types of families are more likely to use drugs; why some intimate relationships fail.

Humans have developed two systems—religion and science—to help them answer the *why* question. These two take very different approaches to knowledge. For religion, faith is the key. The true believer accepts religious teachings despite a lack of concrete, objective evidence. Faith allows us to accept as fact that Moses really did bring the Ten Commandments down from Mount Sinai, that Jesus really did rise from the dead, that Mohammed really was God's prophet.

Science, however, asks us to take little on faith. Science attempts to answer the *why* question by constructing and testing theories. The key test for any theory is whether the theory is supported by concrete, observable, replicable evidence.

I take the latter approach in this text. How does science help us to understand the world around us? Specifically, how can scientific research methods help us to understand families? Let us begin by discussing the stages of social research.

What Are the Stages of Social Research?

Exploration

A basic purpose of social and behavioral research is to find out what, exactly, is going on in society. At some point in any research study, we know little about the phenomenon in which we're interested, and we begin our **exploration.** Because we obviously need to start our research somewhere, we begin by casting a wide net in our search for explanations. We start out with a few ideas about what the phenomenon is or how it works. Perhaps we are curious about what factors are correlated with the birthrate or whether the age at first marriage is increasing or decreasing; or we may need to find out what types of therapies work best for children from abusive households. We often won't have any specific ideas about what key issues we need to study. At this stage in the research process, library research is essential. Before beginning any research project, we need to find out what research has already been done on the topic and what is known (and, more important, what is unknown) about the phenomenon in question. Most of Chapter 3 is devoted to the methods of searching the literature.

Once we have a handle on the existing literature, we might begin our investigation by simple, unscientific observation—watching people going about their daily lives. These preliminary observations are often purely qualitative and interpretive in nature, but from them we can begin to define the problem. What are the key processes and concepts that need to be understood? What aspects of behavior are important? What are the characteristics of the setting or the situation under study? What factor or factors seems to be related to the outcome?

Another way we might begin our research is to ask a small number of people in an unstructured way about their behavior. Let's say that we want to study how new parents make decisions about employment plans. We might begin by identifying a few couples—most likely friends or acquaintances—and talking to them informally about their own experiences. Did the couples have a plan for employment before their children arrived or did they wait until after their children were born to decide who was going to work? What kinds of problems did they encounter in making these decisions? What factors did they consider to decide how much each parent would work outside the home? These discussions can sensitize us to issues we hadn't considered originally. Although this procedure won't produce the most representative sampling of responses, it should help sensitize us to the nature of the problem.

Description

Once we have established some parameters for our research, the next step typically is to formulate a **description** of the characteristics of some group of people or families. What are the characteristics of Asian American families? How do they differ from Latino families? Are educational outcomes for children of employed mothers different from those whose mothers are full-time housewives? Are working-class parents or middle-class parents more likely to use physical punishment? How does the division of household labor change within families over time? These descriptions, although informative, do not tell us why the differences or patterns might exist; they merely assert the possibility of the differences or patterns.

In a *New York Times* (1999, August 31) story headlined "Study Links Teenage Substance Abuse and Paternal Ties," Irwin Molotsky reported that a study conducted by the National Center on Addiction and Substance Abuse found "Teen-agers from one-parent families, typically headed by mothers, are less at risk from tobacco, alcohol and drugs than those in two-parent families who have poor relationships with their fathers." The story seemed to imply that having no father was better than having an uninvolved father. But this study was only a description of the state of affairs; it does not, by itself, provide an explanation for why the father's role is so important. Much research on families is purely descriptive.

In this stage, we are concerned with identifying and labeling phenomena. A good parallel in the biological sciences is the taxonomic classification system of all living organisms into phyla, species, and so forth. The classification system doesn't tell us anything about why living things fall into certain categories; it merely gives a useful structure in which to classify our specimens.

Another important process in this stage is that of **conceptualization,** which involves defining our terms at both the theoretical (abstract) and empirical (concrete) levels. Chapter 5 addresses the issues of conceptualization and measurement.

Explanation

Explanation is specifically concerned with answering the *why* question. Why do families headed by Asian Americans differ from those headed by Hispanics? Why do educational outcomes for children of employed mothers differ from those whose mothers are full-time housewives? Why are working-class parents more likely to use physical punishment than middle-class parents? Why does the division of household labor change within families over time? Here, we go beyond classification and description to explain the phenomena that we have observed.

This process is often the most complex, because meaningful explanations of social and behavioral phenomena require explicit and formal models that show why, of necessity, certain conditions bring about, or are associated with, particular outcomes. We call such a model a **theory.** A theory is a set of logically related statements that claims to explain why, given certain conditions, a specific outcome occurs. Once a theory is confirmed—when it has been shown to account for the phenomena it's supposed to explain—we can then take the theory and use it to predict future outcomes and even to design **interventions** that use the theory's arguments to modify the world around us in a systematic way.

The explanation stage is really about theory construction and testing, a topic that is well beyond the scope of this text. Chafetz (1978) and Reynolds (1971) each presented good introductory treatments of the topic.

Prediction

Although the idea of prediction seems pretty straightforward, it's important to distinguish between predictions, which are based on theory, and *forecasts* or *prophecies*. When the leading investment experts tell us what the stock market is going to do over the next year, they are not typically basing their projections on some body of theory. Although they may be basing their forecast on current and past conditions, we must remember that the past does not predict the future. Teenage marriages aren't more likely to fail simply because they have been more likely to fail in the past. When we observe a particular pattern or relationship among variables repeatedly over time and across populations, it's likely that some real underlying cause produces the observed outcome or effect. There are sound theoretical reasons why teenage marriages have a higher likelihood of divorce, and a good theory should be able to tell us what those reasons are and even under what conditions teenage marriages might be more stable than other marriages.

To predict outcomes, we must know why they happen, which requires theoretical explanation. If we know why certain outcomes occur—that is, if we understand the underlying processes that lead to the outcome in question—we should be able to predict when the outcome will occur and when it will not.

Similarly, just noting that children from single-parent households have lower academic achievement than do other children is not, in and of itself, an explanation of why children from single-parent households do not perform as well in school. It may be that the real causal factor may be something that is related both to family structure and to academic achievement (for example, household income). Or the apparent association between family structure and academic achievement may be a random pattern specific to a particular set of data. The observed association may even be a methodological artifact resulting from flaws in the sampling, data collection, or measurement processes. Without theories to organize our thinking, any speculation about the underlying causes of specific family phenomena is just guesswork.

Interventions

Kurt Lewin said, "There is nothing so practical as a good theory" (Lewin, 1951). If one is truly concerned with changing society, good theory is a necessity. Armed with a good theory, we can design and implement interventions designed to change the world around us. If we really understand why an outcome occurs, we have the knowledge (but not necessarily the resources or technology) to change that outcome. One reason why so many social programs—including those involving children and families—don't seem to work is that they aren't usually based on sound, theoretical knowledge of the process involved. If we have a good theory—one that tells why, of necessity, certain outcomes have to occur given certain conditions—we should have the knowledge necessary to design effective interventions.

Let's consider a concrete example. A theory that might explain the likelihood of a child becoming delinquent depends in part on the amount of time parents spend with that child. If this theory is correct—that is, if the theory is confirmed with empirical evidence—programs that lead parents to be more involved with their children should result in reduced delinquency rates.

Evaluation

Once new programs and policies are in place, it's useful to know whether they really work. Do laws that require jail terms for wife abusers really reduce marital violence? Do stricter divorce laws reduce the rate of divorce? Do subsidies to support additional training of child care providers improve the quality of child care? Even though a theory may have strong confirming evidence to support it, sometimes our social programs—even those based on good theory—don't work. Maybe we didn't implement the program correctly, or maybe the theory is too specific and doesn't work in all situations. In any case, before allocating scarce resources, we need to know whether specific programs work. **Evaluation** of programs and policies tells us whether they are producing the desired types of outcomes or achieving established goals.

In the case of the delinquency project mentioned earlier, we would want to design a careful evaluation of the program's effects. Ideally, this evaluation would be built right into the program itself and not just conducted after the fact. A careful evaluation tells us whether the program really does increase parents' involvement with their children and whether this involvement really does result in decreased rates of delinquent behavior. Chapter 11 focuses on methods of evaluating social programs.

How Is Research on Families Different?

Although the fundamentals of research on families are similar to those of the more general methodologies found in sociology, political science, psychology, and anthropology, important differences exist. For additional discussion of these points, see Gelles (1978) or Larzelere and Klein (1987). The five major differences between research on families and social and behavioral research in general are in the list that follows.

1. Families are systems of individuals.

2. Defining the family is problematic.

3. Family members occupy multiple roles and statuses simultaneously.

4. Much family behavior is private and hidden.

5. We all have preconceptions about families and family life.

Families Are Systems of Individuals

Perhaps the most important difference between research on families and most other research lies in the primary focus of family research: families. In most behavioral and social-science research, the focus is on the individual. If we follow that individual over time, despite marriages, divorces, and job changes, we are still only dealing with a single, identifiable individual. In family research, however, our focus is usually on a *group*—a family—whose composition and characteristics change over time.

Consider a life-course study of a particular married couple. They probably form a family by marrying when both the wife and her husband are in their twenties. Within a few years, they may have children. The couple might divorce at some point, creating two residential groups where there had been only one. Following the divorce, one or both of the spouses might remarry and have children with a new spouse, creating a blended family or stepfamily. One spouse might pass away, leaving a widow or widower. Over time, the children mature and leave home, often to start their own families.

You can see the problem that studying this family presents to a researcher. The composition of the family is constantly changing, sometimes growing, sometimes shrinking. New members enter through the process of birth or marriage and then leave through death or divorce. How can we answer a question as simple as the size of this family when the size is changing over time?

A second problem created by the fact that the family is a system or group of individuals is the **unit of analysis**. Are we focusing on individuals or groups? Is our concern with the marital dyad, the nuclear family, or even the extended family? If we want to measure an individual's social class, we typically look at the person's occupation, education, or income. On the other hand, how do we measure the social class of a family? Is it the husband's characteristics? Or is it the wife's? Do we somehow combine data for both spouses? What about the household income for children of divorced parents?

Do we count only the custodial parent's characteristics, or do we figure in the noncustodial parent's characteristics as well? Even if we decide to limit our analysis to couples (rather than families) we're still not off the hook. Maguire (1999) and Sayer and Klute (2005) present some of the methodological and analytic approaches to handling dyads (couples) as the unit of analysis. I return to the issue of unit of analysis in more detail in Chapter 2.

Defining Family

A fundamental problem in studying families is that we lack a generally agreed-upon definition of what exactly a family is. The U.S. Census Bureau defines a family as a group of two or more people (one of whom is the householder) related by birth, marriage, or adoption and residing together. This definition is unsatisfactory, however, because it excludes many groups that might reasonably be considered families. Are cohabiting couples families? What about gay and lesbian couples? Do foster parents and the children for whom they are responsible constitute families? What about groups living in a communal setting where child care is shared among unrelated adults? Under the U.S. Census Bureau's definition, some groups are considered families even though many observers might disagree. For example, should we define two elderly siblings who live together as a family? Are childless married couples families?

A 1992 national poll by the Roper Organization found that although nearly all respondents (98%) would define a married couple with children as a family, more than 75% also considered an unmarried couple living together and raising children a family; 20% defined two gay men living together as a family, as well. Evidently there are many possible definitions of *family*. This uncertainty about what constitutes a family causes major problems for researchers. Without a generally agreed-upon definition of family, how can researchers know who to study or exclude from their research? Gubrium and Holstein (1990) have discussed these issues in some detail.

Multiple Statuses and Multiple Roles

Gelles pointed out, "Families are made up of individuals occupying multiple statuses and enacting multiple roles" (1978, p. 408). Each member of a family is simultaneously a potential parent, sibling, employee, spouse, and son or daughter. When collecting data about a family member, be sensitive to responses that may depend on which roles and statuses an individual is occupying at the time of the interview. Interviewing adults in the presence of their children, for example, might produce vastly different results than we might obtain by interviewing the same adults in the presence of their own parents.

Backstage Behavior

Another problem in studying families is the fact that much of what goes on in families is what is known as *backstage behavior* (hidden from public view). Important behaviors such as child abuse, domestic violence, and child rearing are not generally visible to persons outside the family. Until recently, for example, the rate of domestic violence was widely believed to be relatively low. As better research produced higher-quality data, social scientists realized that because incidents of domestic violence are often known only to members of the family and perhaps close friends, rates of such behavior can be grossly underestimated.

There is another problem related to this backstage behavior. "Families develop private, idiosyncratic norms and meanings about their own activities" (Larzelere & Klein, 1987, p. 135). Each family has its own patterns of, and rules for, behavior. Often these are the result of years (or even generations) of living together. Think about your own family: Aren't there unwritten rules about who sits where at the dinner table or a pecking order for seats in the family automobile? Often, these rules are not shared with the outside world, and a researcher studying the family may not be privy to these secrets.

Families even have ways of restructuring the way they view themselves to fit these rules and expectations. In *The Second Shift,* Hochschild and Machung talk about "family myths" that are "versions of reality that obscure a family truth in order to manage a family tension" (1989, p. 19). One couple explained that they "shared" the housework by dividing the house into an upstairs and a downstairs. The wife was responsible for all the tasks associated with the upstairs, which included the kitchen, living areas, bedrooms, and bathrooms. The husband's downstairs responsibilities covered the garage and activities such as auto maintenance, yard work, and general household repairs.

In response to the interviewer's questioning, both husband and wife presented this housework "sharing" as an equitable solution to the division of household labor, even though an outside observer might think the arrangement was anything but fair or equitable. The public image that a family chooses to present to the outside world can be different from the private, internal image.

Preconceptions About the Family

Another problem that interferes with our ability to study families is that everyone is familiar with families; we all have ideas about what are right, good, or appropriate family behaviors and structures. If you study invertebrate zoology, you are unlikely to have strong beliefs about worms and insects; when you sit down to study French philosophy, you probably don't have strong feelings one way or another about Voltaire or Descartes. That's not the case with the issues that family researchers study, however. We all have attitudes and beliefs about topics such as premarital sex, abortion, same-sex marriage, extramarital affairs, day care, corporal punishment, the employ-ment of mothers of young children, and the allocation of household chores. It's difficult for us to study such phenomena without our own beliefs intruding into the analysis.

These preconceptions take at least three forms. First, our own back-grounds may *bias* us in favor of or against certain forms of family behavior. People whose own mothers were employed outside the home, for example, are more likely to approve of the employment of mothers of young children. Members of certain religious groups are more prone to oppose legalized abor-tion than are members of other groups. Political conservatives are more apt to emphasize the importance of the husband's dominance of the marriage relationship than are political liberals.

Second, our own experiences can serve as limits to what we know or understand. Most middle-class people have little contact with welfare recipi-ents, for example, so they may not have much sympathy for, or understand-ing of, people who use and need the social welfare system. Christians in this country have relatively little firsthand experience with religious discrimina-tion and may not be sensitive to the messages they send to non-Christians when they conduct religious pageants in public settings.

A third factor that leads to preconceptions about the family has to do with *ethnocentrism*, which is the belief that the ideas and practices of our own ethnicity, gender, or social class are somehow *the best* or *right*. Sociologists remind us that we need to be aware of the multiple and intersecting effects of race, social class, and gender. Most of the family phenomena we study differ by race—compare the family structures of white and African American families, for example. And family behavior varies by social class. One of the best-known phenomenon in the study of child rearing is that the use of corporal punishment is highest among working-class families and lowest among upper-class families. We must also recognize that the family is a highly gendered environment. Much of what goes on in families varies by gender: who does which tasks around the house, who cares for the children, who is the primary breadwinner, educational and career expectations for the children, and so forth.

When we study families, we cannot simply ignore these preconceptions. We need to be aware that our own beliefs may affect the topics we choose to study and the methods we use to study those topics. As difficult as it is, we need to take care to design our studies so that our biases don't influence the results or our interpretations of those results.

The Benefits of Well-Conducted Research

By this point you have probably reached the conclusion that doing quality research on children and families is not an easy task. You're right; it's a lot of work to design and execute a research project that will yield solid, meaningful findings. And we are bombarded daily by the results of poor research. Do you really trust the results of a telephone opinion poll in which respondents have to pay 50 cents to give their opinions or a survey of likely voters run by a candidate's own campaign organization?

So, why is it important to do good research?

First, as I suggested in the beginning of this chapter, the familiarity of the family often makes it difficult to explain general family processes and theories to laypersons. When I talk about my research on families to groups outside the university, the audiences react with, "Sure, I knew that." However, the fact that a particular research finding makes sense does not make it any less important.

A second problem is that what seems obvious at first glance often isn't so obvious after all. I know a popular media device is to make fun of researchers who study behaviors and relationships that are obvious to everybody. However, that which is obvious is not always true. For example, it's obvious that older Americans are more likely to be victims of violent crime than are younger people, right? Older people are more vulnerable and easier targets for thieves. Yet, exactly the opposite is true: Americans older than the age of 65 years are approximately one-sixth as likely to be victims of violent crime as is the general population (U.S. Bureau of the Census, 2004, p. 195).

Another obvious relationship is the effect of cohabitation experience on marital stability. It makes sense that those who have lived together before marriage should have a lower chance of divorce; presumably, cohabitants learn relationship skills that they can use to improve the quality of their marriages. However, this does not seem to be the case. Research suggests that (a) women who cohabited with their husbands before marriage were approximately 50% more likely than noncohabitants to have their marriages disrupted, and (b) those who cohabited with someone other than their eventual husband were more than twice as likely to experience separation or divorce as those who didn't cohabit (Bumpass, Martin, & Sweet, 1991).

Complicating these issues is that some aspects of family life such as births, divorces, and marriages are easy to observe and measure, but others including child abuse, marital happiness, and family dynamics are difficult to measure in any objective way. Sometimes I like to think of the study of the family as a *hard science* because it's so much harder to do research on marriages, families, and children than it is to study electrons, microbes, or chemical reactions.

One crucial reason we need quality research on families is rooted in our motivation for choosing to study families. If you're like me, one of the reasons you're interested in studying families is because you'd like to bring about change. You might see neglected children and hope to see them in homes where they will get lots of love and attention. Or you might want to help unhappy married couples communicate with and respect each other. Perhaps you want to help abusive husbands deal constructively with their anger (or maybe you just want to lock them up and throw away the key). To accomplish these goals, you need the best, most objective information available—the kind of information you'll get from quality research.

Study Questions

1. Find and briefly describe examples of published research on families at each of the six stages of social research (exploration, description, explanation, prediction, intervention, and evaluation).

2. List as many of the roles and/or statuses that you occupy in life as you can. Give an example of one of these roles or statuses (for example, *employee* or *student*) that conflicts with a family-related role or status (for example, *spouse* or *parent*). How do you deal with or resolve this conflict?

3. Ask three friends or acquaintances to define *family*. Discuss the similarities and differences between their definitions. Give examples of groups that would be considered *families* under one or two of the definitions but not the other(s). How might these definitions affect the way one would do research on families?

4. Choose some aspect of families that interests you (for example, child well-being, division of household labor, marital stability, or fathers' involvement with children), and give three examples of how a researcher's preconceptions or personal opinions might affect the way that research is done on that topic.

5. From your own family, give an example of a *family myth*—something that is generally accepted to be real or true even though some or all of your family members know that it isn't. Why do you think your family has created this family myth?

6. Even though most people think older Americans are more likely to be victims of crime than younger people, research shows that this is untrue. Find a published study on a family-related topic that reports a finding that is contrary to the conventional wisdom. Why do you think that people accept this conventional *wisdom*?

For Further Reading

Bumpass, L. L., Martin, T. C., & Sweet, J. A. (1991). The impact of family background and early marital factors on marital disruption. *Journal of Family Issues, 12,* 22–42.

Chafetz, J. S. (1978). *A primer on the construction and testing of theories in sociology.* Itasca, IL: F. E. Peacock.

Gelles, R. J. (1978). Methods for studying sensitive family topics. *American Journal of Orthopsychiatry, 48,* 408–424.

Gubrium, J. F., & Holstein, J. A. (1990). *What is family?* Mountain View, CA: Mayfield.

Hochschild, A. R., & Machung, A. (1989). *The second shift.* New York: Viking.

Larzelere, R., & Klein, D. M. (1987). Methodology. In M. B. Sussman & S. K. Steinmetz (Eds.), *Handbook of marriage and the family* (pp. 126–156). New York: Plenum.

Lewin, K. (1951). *Field theory in social science; selected theoretical papers.* D. Cartwright (Ed.). New York: Harper & Row.

Maguire, M. C. (1999). Treating the dyad as the unit of analysis: A primer on three analytic approaches. *Journal of Marriage and the Family, 61,* 213–223.

Molotsky, I. (1999, August 31). Study links teenage substance abuse and paternal ties. *New York Times,* A16.

Reynolds, P. D. (1971). *A primer on theory construction.* Indianapolis: Bobbs-Merrill.

Sayer, A. G., & Klute, M. M. (2005). Analyzing couples and families: Multilevel methods. In V. L. Bengtson, A. C. Acock, K. R. Allen, P. Dilworth-Anderson, & D. M. Klein (Eds.), *Sourcebook of family theory and research* (pp. 289–313). Thousand Oaks, CA: Sage.

U.S. Bureau of the Census. (2004). *Statistical abstract of the United States* (115th ed.). Washington, DC: Bureau of the Census.

2

Causal Inference in Family Research

Much of our thinking about families is framed in terms of causality. When we see an outcome—spousal abuse, divorce, increasing age at first marriage, smaller family sizes—a reasonable first question is, "What is causing this outcome?" Implicitly, we are attempting to answer the *why* question in terms of cause and effect: We know the effect, but what is the cause?

To think causally, we must first identify several types of variables that may appear in our analysis. Family size, age at marriage, and marital satisfaction are all variables because they vary. Our analyses involve variables and their attributes, values, states, or levels. Is a particular respondent male or female? Here, gender is a variable with two levels or attributes: male and female. Does the United States have a high or low median age at marriage? Age at marriage is a variable because it can take on many different values, ranging from young to relatively old age at first marriage.

We usually label variables in terms of their **theoretical roles** in our research. Variables typically occupy one of four major theoretical roles in family research: independent, dependent, intervening (mediator or mediating), and control (moderator or moderating) variables.

Variables

Dependent Variables

In research terms, we think of the outcome or the effect as the **dependent variable.** A dependent variable is the factor or characteristic that we think is caused, produced, or affected by some other factors. If we are studying factors affecting marital satisfaction, marital satisfaction is the dependent variable in the analysis.

Independent Variables

A factor that causes, affects, or produces changes in the dependent variable is known as an **independent variable.** For example, if we think that age at marriage somehow affects marital satisfaction, age at marriage is the independent variable in the analysis.

A Simple Causal Model

We now have a simple causal model to consider. We think that through some process, age at marriage affects marital satisfaction. We can conceptualize this relationship in many different ways. For example, we could say that

Figure 2.1   Effects of Age at Marriage on Marital Satisfaction

age at marriage affects how satisfied people are with their marriages, or we could suggest that those in marriages in which the spouses were teenagers when they married will have lower levels of marital satisfaction than those in marriages in which the bride and groom were in their thirties. In either case, we could diagram this simple causal model as is shown in Figure 2.1.

The independent variable (age at marriage) is on the left-hand side of the diagram, and the dependent variable (marital satisfaction) is on the right-hand side. We generally diagram causal relationships from left to right, proceeding from the most fundamental independent variable on the left to the dependent variable of interest on the right. The arrow connecting the two variables is pointed at marital satisfaction, indicating that our model suggests that age at marriage causes or affects marital satisfaction. The plus sign (+) over that line indicates a positive relationship between age at marriage and marital satisfaction; that is, older ages at marriage are associated with higher levels of marital satisfaction, and younger ages at marriage are associated with lower levels of marital satisfaction. A negative relationship (one in which higher levels of the independent variable are associated with lower levels of the dependent variable, and vice versa) would be indicated by a minus sign (–).

Notice in the diagram that we didn't label the dependent variable as high marital satisfaction or low marital satisfaction or the independent variable as teenagers or early twenties. It's important to distinguish between variables themselves and states, levels, or categories of those variables. As an example, let's say we had a model that studies differences between men's and women's scores on standardized tests. The independent variable here wouldn't be male or female; it would be gender.

Intervening (Mediator or Mediating) Variables

This is a simplified model, and nobody really believes that age at marriage is the only variable that affects marital satisfaction. It's possible that age at marriage affects some other variable, which in turn affects marital satisfaction. In this case, that other variable is an **intervening variable** or a **mediator** (or mediating) **variable.** For example, age at marriage might affect emotional

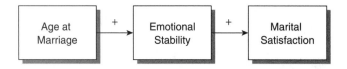

Figure 2.2   Effects of Age at Marriage on Marital Satisfaction With Mediating (Intervening) Variable

stability—because younger people are less emotionally stable than older ones are—and emotional stability, in turn, might affect marital satisfaction. Our causal model now looks like Figure 2.2.

The diagram clarifies that our model doesn't suggest that age at marriage affects marital satisfaction directly. Rather, our model says that the effects of age at marriage (our independent variable) on marital satisfaction (our dependent variable) are mediated by emotional stability (intervening variable). In other words, this model says that one's age at marriage affects one's emotional stability, and emotional stability, in turn, affects one's marital satisfaction.

This addition of an intervening variable to our model is important because it tells us a great deal about the process through which age at marriage affects marital satisfaction. It tells us, for example, that not all people who marry at an early age will have low levels of marital satisfaction (young people who are emotionally stable should not have substantially lower marital satisfaction). Similarly, it also tells us that we would expect people who were emotionally unstable to have lower levels of marital satisfaction, regardless of how old they were when they married.

Moderating (Control or Moderator) Variables

Sometimes our theories suggest that the effect of the independent variable on the dependent variable is different for different groups. For example, let's assume that our theory tells us that age at marriage affects marital satisfaction for Protestants and Jews (that is, the younger Protestants or Jews are when they marry, the lower their marital satisfaction), but age at marriage doesn't affect marital satisfaction for Catholics. What's the role of religious affiliation in this model? In terms of a diagram, it would look like Figure 2.3.

Note that this model doesn't suggest that religious affiliation affects age at marriage; if it did, the arrow coming out of the religious-affiliation box would be pointing at the age-at-marriage box. And it also doesn't argue that religious affiliation affects marital satisfaction. What this model tells us is that religious affiliation affects the relationship between age at marriage and marital satisfaction (and not either variable individually).

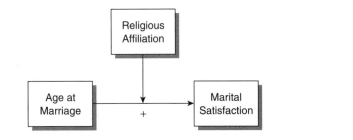

Figure 2.3   Effects of Age at Marriage on Marital Satisfaction With
Moderating (Control) Variable

In this model, religious affiliation is a **control variable** or **moderator** (or moderating) **variable**. In this case, we call it a moderator variable because religious affilation moderates or changes the relationship between the independent variable (age at marriage) and the dependent variable (marital satisfaction). Control- or moderating-variable effects are among the most interesting findings in social research because they suggest that the phenomenon under study works differently for different groups or different types of individuals or families. Such knowledge can lead us to a better understanding of how, exactly, the process works. Why, for example, should age at marriage affect marital satisfaction for Protestants and Jews but not Catholics? The case might be that Catholics have historically married at younger ages than Protestants and Jews; because early marriage is a normatively approved behavior among Catholics, it doesn't have the effect on marital satisfaction that it does for members of other religious groups. Baron and Kenny (1986) presented an excellent treatment of the importance of the moderator and mediator variable in causal models.

Two other uses of the term *control variable* bear mentioning here. Sometimes, other variables affect the dependent variable, even though we aren't specifically interested in their effects. For example, we know from previous research that age at marriage is the best single predictor of marital stability. Even if we were primarily interested in the effects of some other variable—say, the wife's employment status—we still want to include age at first marriage in our model. Most statistical techniques allow for the inclusion of such control variables, and permit us to see the effects of our independent variable of interest (in this case, the wife's employment) controlling for, or net of, the effects of other variables in the model, including age at first marriage. In principle, one can include as many of these control variables in the model as needed, but generally it is considered inappropriate to include this type of control variable without reasonable evidence to suggest that it affects the dependent variable. This type of model is depicted in Figure 2.4.

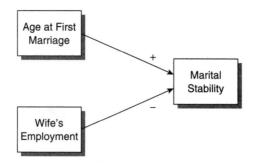

Figure 2.4   Effects of Age at Marriage and Wife's Employment on Marital
Stability

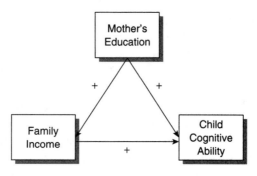

Figure 2.5   Effects of Family Income and Mother's Education on Child
Cognitive Ability

Another type of control variable is one that affects both the independent
variable and the dependent variable. In research on child well-being, for
example, it is often hypothesized that family income has an effect on child
cognitive ability: All things being equal, children from higher-income families
tend to have higher levels of cognitive ability than do children from lower-
income families. However, mother's education probably affects both the independent variable (family income) and the dependent variable (child cognitive
ability). Again, we would probably want to include mother's education in any
statistical model so that the effects of family income on child cognitive ability
(controlling for, or net of, the effects of mother's education) can be assessed
(shown in Figure 2.5).

Before leaving the subject of the theoretical role of variables, I should point out that just because a given variable occupies a particular theoretical role in one study doesn't mean that it can't occupy a different theoretical role in another study. For example, age at marriage is the independent variable in the marital stability study described here. In a different study, age at marriage might be a dependent variable. For instance, a researcher might want to see how parents' education and income affect the marital-timing decisions of their children. Although a few variables (race and gender are good examples) are unlikely to be anything but independent variables (what variables, after all, affect one's race or gender?) most variables can occupy different theoretical roles in different studies.

Units of Analysis

In most social and behavioral research, the **unit of analysis** is the individual: Data are collected from and about individual persons. Although these individuals can be combined into groups (for example, all college-educated individuals, or all individuals older than the age of 65 years) the focus is on the individual. In family research, however, we deal with many different units of analysis. Larzelere and Klein (1987) suggested that family research deals with (a) data on dyads (couples), coresidential families, and extended families; (b) data aggregated at various levels (for example, community-level data, statewide data, and data at the national level); and (c) data on individuals. The discussion that follows and the accompanying table borrow heavily from their work and that of Levinger and Raush (1977).

In Table 2.1, analyses that examine the effects of individual-level characteristics on other individual-level characteristics are represented in cell 1,1. For example, a study of how personal income affects marriage timing would examine the effects of an individual-level independent variable on an individual-level dependent variable. If our theory hypothesized that regional economic conditions (for example, the unemployment rate) affected the rate of domestic violence, however, we would be examining the effects of a variable at the aggregate level (regional unemployment rate) on a measure taken at the coresidential family level represented in the table by cell 5,3.

Family research often examines the effects of variables measured at the dyadic, coresidential family, extended family, and aggregate levels on individual-level or coresidential family outcomes. For example, we might study the effects of family social class (measured at the level of the coresidential family) on sons' occupational aspirations (an individual-level variable); this type of analysis fits in cell 3,1. Less commonly, research might examine the

Table 2.1   A Matrix for Generating Research Questions About Families

Unit of Analysis: Independent Variable	Unit of Analysis: Dependent Variable			
	1. Individual	*2. Dyad*	*3. Coresidential Family*	*4. Extended Family*
1. Individual	1,1	1,2	1,3	1,4
2. Dyad	2,1	2,2	2,3	2,4
3. Coresidential Family	3,1	3,2	3,3	3,4
4. Extended Family	4,1	4,2	4,3	4,4
5. Aggregate Level	5,1	5,2	5,3	5,4

effect of individual-level variables on measures taken at the coresidential or extended family levels. Whatever the unit of analysis, the research design must be sensitive to the fact that (unlike most social and behavioral research, which focuses on individuals as the unit of analysis) data can be gathered on many different levels.

Thinking Causally

Few problems in the philosophy of science have stirred so much interest as the issue of cause and effect. This is particularly true in the social and behavioral sciences, because often the primary concern is with how to bring about change in some dependent variable. If a theory claims that some independent variable really causes some dependent variable, that suggests that changes in the independent variable should produce changes in the dependent variable. For example, if the amount of parental supervision has a **causal effect** on delinquent behavior, increasing the amount of parental supervision should result in decreases in delinquent behavior.

But how do we know when we really have a causal effect? No doubt you've heard the saying, "Correlation does not imply causation," meaning that simply because two variables seem to be associated with each other doesn't mean that one of them causes the other. To take an example, imagine that a researcher has gathered data on family violence (the dependent variable) and is searching for factors that might be causally related to it. The researcher has data on the number of incidents of family violence in major American cities on a monthly basis. By coincidence, the researcher also has monthly data on ice cream consumption in those same cities.

Figure 2.6   Effects of Ice Cream Consumption on Rate of Family Violence
(Spurious Relationship)

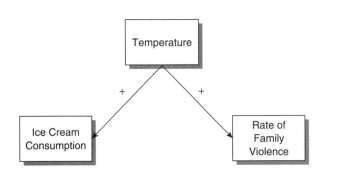

Figure 2.7   Effects of Temperature on Ice Cream Consumption and Rate of
Family Violence (Nonspurious Relationship)

To her surprise, the researcher finds that the number of incidents of family
violence is correlated with ice cream consumption. The number of incidents of
family violence is lowest when ice cream consumption is low and highest when
ice cream consumption is at its peak. Could some ingredient in ice cream possibly make people want to assault their spouses? That is, does consumption of
ice cream causally affect the rate of family violence?

You've probably already figured out what's going on here. Both the rate
of family violence and the consumption of ice cream are affected by a third
variable: weather (or, more specifically, the temperature). The rate of family
violence and the consumption of ice cream both peak during the warm sum-
mer months, and are both at their lowest point during the winter. This relationship is diagrammed like the model in Figure 2.7.

This is a classic example of what is known as a **spurious effect.** What
initially appeared to be a causal effect of ice cream consumption on family
violence is, in fact, caused by the effects of a third variable—temperature—
on both the independent and dependent variables. Ice cream consumption
has no causal effect on family violence, even though the research may show
a correlation or association between the two. In Figure 2.7, notice that there
is no line representing a causal effect that connects the variables ice cream

consumption and rate of family violence. This is because in the revised model, the influence of temperature on both ice cream consumption and family violence creates the spurious effect.

How do we determine if an association or relationship is causal, as opposed to spurious? There are three main conditions that must be met if an effect is to be judged causal: temporal precedence, constant conjunction, and nonspuriousness.

Temporal Precedence

If X causes Y, then X must precede Y in time. Obviously, X can't be a cause of Y if X happens after Y. In the age-at-marriage/marital-satisfaction example, age at marriage precedes marital satisfaction, so the temporal precedence requirement is met.

Constant Conjunction

If X causes Y, then X and Y have to be highly associated or correlated with each other. If age at marriage really affects marital satisfaction, then age at marriage should be highly associated with marital satisfaction—not just in one or a few studies, but in many studies over time. In this case, it is well-known that the relationship of age at marriage to marital satisfaction is consistent in nearly every study of marriages, so the constant conjunction requirement is met.

Nonspuriousness

Clearly, if the effect of the independent variable on the dependent variable is attributable to some spurious process, that effect can't be causal. Consider the possibility that there may be some variable that affects both age at marriage and marital satisfaction. Maybe some personality trait leads people to both marry early and have unstable marriages. If such a trait exists, it may be the case that the effect of age at marriage on marital satisfaction is spurious, not causal.

To conclude that a relationship or effect is truly causal, we have to be able to eliminate the possibility that there is some variable (or group of variables) that affects both the independent and dependent variables producing the appearance of a causal effect when in fact the relationship is spurious. To do this, the researcher has to do three things:

1. The researcher has to identify the variables that are producing the spurious effect.

2. The researcher has to have empirical data on those variables.

3. The researcher has to perform the appropriate statistical analyses to determine whether the relationship appears to be spurious.

Of these three, the first is usually the most difficult. Potentially, there are thousands of variables that might be creating a spurious effect in any particular analysis. Usually, speculation is limited to those variables linked, by a conceptual or theoretical relationship, to the independent and dependent variables in our analysis. Although eliminating all potential sources of spurious effects is probably impossible, we need to eliminate at least the most plausible sources of spuriousness before claiming that the effects are causal.

I will discuss statistical procedures further later in this text. Now that we know something about different types of variables and causality, we're ready to frame a research hypothesis.

Framing the Hypothesis

Most family research begins with a **hypothesis.** A hypothesis is a forecast or expectation about how variables are associated or how they are causally related. For example, one hypothesis that might be framed about the relationship between age at marriage and marital satisfaction is "Age at marriage has a positive effect on marital satisfaction."

This hypothesis suggests that, all things being equal, people who marry at younger ages will tend to have lower levels of marital satisfaction, whereas those who marry later in life will tend to have higher levels of marital satisfaction. This hypothesis does not mean that every person who marries at an early age will have an unhappy marriage, nor that every person who marries later in life will have a happy marriage. Research hypotheses are typically framed in terms of group averages and tendencies—not the behavior of specific individuals.

Where do hypotheses come from? Ideally, they should come from theories, because the unambiguous logical structure of a good theory tells us why, of necessity, a particular independent variable causes or is associated with a particular dependent variable. Practically speaking, however, because relatively few such theories exist in the study of the family, most hypotheses come from either reading the existing body of research literature or from common sense or intuition.

Directional Hypotheses

Hypotheses typically take one of two forms. The framed-at-age hypothesis is a **directional hypothesis,** because it states an expectation about the direction of the relationship between the independent variable and the dependent variable. Increased age at marriage is hypothesized to have a positive effect on marital satisfaction, meaning that those who marry at an early age are expected to have the lowest levels of marital satisfaction, and those who marry at somewhat older ages are expected to have higher levels of marital satisfaction. It follows that age at marriage usually has a negative effect on likelihood of divorce: Those who are younger when they marry are more likely to have unstable marriages, whereas those who are older when they marry are less likely to have unstable marriages.

Nondirectional Hypotheses

In a **nondirectional hypothesis,** the independent variable has an association with, or effect on, the dependent variable, but there is insufficient information to allow an intelligent guess about the direction of that relationship. For example, we might hypothesize that income will affect marital satisfaction, but without some body of knowledge to inform us whether high-income persons will be more (or less) satisfied with their marriages than low-income persons, our hypothesis remains nondirectional.

Whatever the source or structure of the hypothesis, however, it is important to be able to defend it against the critics. You should always be able to justify your hypothesis in terms of theory, existing research, or some type of logical argument. The burden of proof is always on the researcher to demonstrate that the hypothesis is reasonable and that it follows logically from previous theory or research.

Study Questions

1. Choose two family-related variables and (a) give brief definitions of both variables and (b) identify the states, levels, or attributes of both variables.

2. Choose a research article from a family-related journal and identify the independent, dependent, moderating (if any), and intervening (if any) variables in the conceptual model. Draw a causal diagram representing the conceptual model.

3. Choose a variable of interest to you, and present a conceptual model that shows that variable as an independent variable. Then repeat the process with three more models that show that variable as a dependent, moderating, and mediating variable, respectively. Draw a causal diagram for each. Note: Because not all variables (race and gender are good examples) can occupy all the different theoretical roles, you should choose your variable carefully.

4. Describe a relationship in the family literature that appears to be a causal effect but is in fact spurious. Clearly identify the variables involved and draw a causal diagram representing this process.

5. Choose some process or relationship in the family literature and frame a hypothesis about that process or relationship. Clearly identify the independent and dependent variables in your hypothesis, and the direction (if appropriate) of the relationship.

For Further Reading

Baron, R. M., & Kenny, D. A. (1986). The moderator-mediator variable distinction in social-psychological research: Conceptual, strategic, and statistical considerations. *Journal of Personal and Social Psychology, 51,* 1173–1182.

Larzelere, R., & Klein, D. M. (1987). Methodology. In M. B. Sussman & S. K. Steinmetz (Eds.), *Handbook of marriage and the family* (pp. 126–156). New York: Plenum.

Levinger, G., & Raush, H. L. (1977). *Close relationships: Perspectives on the meaning of intimacy.* Amherst: University of Massachusetts Press.

3

Searching and Reading the Literature

O nce you've selected a topic to study (and identified at least the dependent variable), you need to examine the prior research literature on your topic. It's always surprising to me that people think that they're the first to be interested in a particular topic. I get phone calls from people who want to conduct a study of some family-related phenomenon—say, first-time mothers returning to work—who assume that nobody has ever studied the topic before. The fact of the matter is that in any given year, several thousand studies relating to families and children are published. So, regardless of whether you're planning a study of your own or you simply want to know what's already been done, you need to begin by searching the literature.

Although some of this research is published as research monographs (what most of us think of as books), most research on families and children is published as articles in professional journals. *Journal of Marriage and the Family, Journal of Family Issues, Child Development, Developmental Psychology, Journal of Family Psychology,* and *Family Relations* are some of the best-known journals specializing in research on families and children.

To find out what research has been published on a given topic, you'll need to search these and other journals. Because scholars who do research on families may have backgrounds in sociology, psychology, and other fields, the articles you seek might be published in sociological journals, psychological journals, or other sources. Fortunately, there are several excellent indexing systems available to take much of the work out of this task. *Sociological Abstracts* indexes virtually all the sociological journals, whereas *PsycINFO* indexes publications in psychology. A third indexing system is *Social Science Citation Index* (SSCI), which scans journals across the social sciences. SSCI is distinct in that it reports how frequently a given article is cited by other research, thus giving a crude measure of the *impact* of a particular article on the discipline.

Although the exact details of using these indexing systems vary, the general procedures are similar. Your local reference librarian can show you the specifics of how to access these services in your library. Many libraries also make these services available to their patrons over the Internet.

There are also indexing systems specifically for literature on family research. The *Family Studies Database* is the electronic version of *Inventory of Marriage and Family Literature* and *FAMILY (Australian Family & Society Abstracts)*. It indexes more than 1,800 journals, books, chapters, newsletters, government documents, and dissertations and covers the educational, medical, psychological, and sociological aspects of family literature.

Whichever index system you select, begin by choosing some keywords that are appropriate for the research that you're seeking. For example, if you wanted to study the relationship of child abuse to school performance, the keywords might include *child abuse, academic outcomes,* and *school.* You probably will want to review any articles listed under child abuse and either academic outcomes or school. Once these keywords are entered, the software will display a list of journal articles that studied these issues. If this step generates dozens of references, you probably need to narrow your focus by adding additional keywords as limitations on the search. If you get only a few references, however, the search keywords probably are inappropriate and you need to change them.

The next step is to read the articles' abstracts. An **abstract** is a brief summary of what a study was about, how the research was conducted, and what the findings were. As you read these abstracts (which are typically displayed along with the reference items by the indexing software) you will find that only some of the articles are really relevant to your work. You will probably then want to find the actual journal containing the articles and scan the articles to see if they are indeed relevant. Sometimes journals publish a **review article,** which summarizes the research literature on a particular topic. Such articles will save you a lot of work, because much of the pertinent literature will already be cited and summarized for you. You may want to photocopy the most important articles so that you won't have to go to the library every time you need to work on your project.

Reading a Journal Article

Once you're satisfied that you have the most important articles about your topic, sit down and read them in detail. Articles in professional journals may be unlike anything you've read before. They are concisely written—journal articles are rarely longer than 25 pages—and they tend to use many abbreviations, technical terms, and jargon. Fortunately, they follow a rather strict style with a number of clearly defined sections. The following discussion of the various sections of a typical journal article will help you to read the articles you've located and write your own research article.

Title

Of course, each article has a title, and the content of the title is highly informative. It will probably identify the dependent and independent variables and perhaps the nature of who was studied. For example, a title such as "Effects of Age at Marriage on Marital Satisfaction Among Asian American Women" immediately tells you that the independent variable is age at marriage, the dependent variable is marital satisfaction, and Asian American women were studied.

Author and Institutional Affiliation

Immediately below the title will be any author names and their institutional affiliations. You'll notice university faculty members write most of the research articles.

Abstract

As I mentioned earlier, an abstract is a brief summary of the research study. It should include the primary hypotheses, the nature of the sample, a brief mention of the research procedures and analyses, a brief statement of the findings, and a sentence about the implications of the study—all in 150 to 200 words. Always read the abstract first—if the article isn't relevant to your interests, you can save yourself a lot of time.

Introduction

The introduction section (which typically will not have a heading indicating as much) introduces the problem and justifies its importance. This section should answer the question "Why should anyone care about this problem?" On one hand, the importance of the paper might be justified in practical or policy terms. For example, in my 1990 paper "Marital Disruption and the Employment of Married Women," I point out that because people have long associated the employment of married women with an increased risk of divorce, it is important to know if this relationship, in fact, exists (Greenstein, 1990). In other words, I argue that the topic is important and worth studying because of its practical significance.

On the other hand, an author may argue that a paper is important because of its theoretical or conceptual significance. In "Gender, Labor Allocations, and the Psychology of Entitlement Within the Home," Sanchez (1994) explicitly sought to use several different theoretical traditions to explain how women and men perceive fairness of the division of household labor. Although there may be indirect policy or practical implications of the research, the paper was aimed primarily at an application of theories.

Generally speaking, a research article might be published for any of several reasons. First, it's possible that a particular problem has never been studied. Assuming that the problem is one of interest to those studying families, the article will fill a gap in the research literature.

Second, it's possible that, although the particular problem has been studied, the author finds shortcomings or problems in the existing literature. For example, the author might offer methodological improvements over previous research—perhaps with a better sample or more precise measurement.

Previous research might have methodological flaws that the author claims a new study can correct; sometimes incorrect statistical procedures or biased instruments can produce faulty or misleading conclusions. Also, previous research might contain conceptual flaws; perhaps the author feels that a different theoretical approach is necessary or that a previous author incorrectly applied some body of theory. An article might **replicate** previous research in a different population with more recent data, better controls, or better measures of key variables.

Regardless of how the authors choose to justify the importance of the paper, their goal is to convince the reader that the topic is worth studying. The introduction should convince the reader that the problem under study is important and should indicate where the authors are going in the article, how they're going to get there, and why the research is being done.

Literature Review

Again, there may not be a *literature review* heading, but at some point, the authors discuss previous studies relevant to the current research. There is a simple rule for which items should be discussed in the literature review: Discuss all that is relevant and nothing that isn't. The authors will want to include the major studies that have looked at the same independent and dependent variables as their study. It's unnecessary to cite every study ever conducted on the topic—only the important ones. The authors' goal in the literature review is not only to show what's already been done on the topic, but more important, to show what hasn't been done and why their study must be done.

If the authors have hypotheses to present, they will usually immediately follow the literature review. The hypotheses should be stated as explicitly as possible. Often, hypotheses are stated first in conceptual or abstract terms, then in concrete or operational terms. The hypotheses should tell exactly which outcomes will confirm (be consistent with) the hypotheses and which outcomes will disconfirm (be inconsistent with) the hypotheses.

Methods

There will probably be a section labeled *methods* or *methodology* (the term should usually be methods, because methodology is the study of method, and what the author is presenting here is a description of a method, not the study of methods). The purpose of this section is twofold: first, to describe exactly who was studied (the sample) and how they were studied (the procedures); and second, to describe what was studied (the measurements or instruments).

Ideally, this section should provide enough information for the reader to judge whether the sample and procedures were appropriate for the problem and the outcomes.

Sample

Nearly all methods sections will begin with a discussion of the sample. This should tell the reader exactly who was studied, how many were studied (the sample size), when the data were gathered, how respondents were selected, and so forth. If another researcher or organization originally collected the data (for example, the U.S. Census Bureau), there should be a citation to the original source documentation for the data.

Measurement

This subsection should identify all the key variables in the study and explain how they were operationalized or measured. If sample surveys were used, this section should provide the exact wording of key items or questions that are used in the study. If standardized scales or indices were used, this subsection should cite the original sources and briefly report any known problems with validity or reliability of the measures. Any recoded items (categories combined for analytic purposes) should be clarified.

For qualitative studies, this section can be problematic. Many qualitative studies are exploratory in nature; it's not always clear what the key variables are or how they should be measured. Rather, this information may emerge from the data collection process.

Procedures

This subsection should explain in detail exactly how the data were gathered. There are two main purposes of this subsection: first, to describe exactly what techniques were used to collect the data; and second, to provide enough detail to allow an interested researcher to replicate the study.

Findings or Results

Sometimes this section will be labeled *analyses*. The actual results of the study should be reported here without interpretation (interpretation of the results follow in the *discussion* section). The beginning of this section should consider general issues such as response rates and estimates of reliability and validity. Any statistical techniques used should be described here and their use justified. The authors must convince the reader that their techniques were appropriate and the best available for the particular types of data and research questions. If the techniques were unusual or are not commonly used, the authors may take a few paragraphs to explain them.

In most quantitative studies, the first results reported will be descriptive statistics about the respondents. Typically, the analyses will include a table of statistics about the variables in the analyses. This table is important because it tells the reader much about the characteristics of the respondents in the study: Age, gender, race, education, marital status, and other relevant variables are typically reported. Other tables will probably report results relating to the hypotheses or goals of the study. Additional information about tables follows.

Discussion

The *discussion* section usually begins with a restatement of the research problem followed by a listing of the major hypotheses. Next, the evidence supporting the hypotheses will be presented and interpreted. Any weaknesses or problems with the design of the study or the quality of the data should be mentioned and explained. For example, the data might be relatively old, or the sample might be unusual or biased in some way. Perhaps it was not possible to control for some important explanatory variable. These issues need to be made clear to the reader, and the authors will generally try to show why these concerns don't interfere with their ability to draw reasonable inferences from the study.

Any alternative interpretations of the findings—that is, different ways of interpreting the results—should be discussed. All findings should be related back to previous theory or research with the emphasis on how the research accomplished the goals set out in the beginning of the introduction. If the conclusions of the article are not presented in a separate section, they are normally at the end of the discussion section.

Conclusions

The *conclusion* is the wrap-up of the article where the authors tell us what they have contributed to the literature. They may also link the research findings to specific social-policy issues or to further developments in theory. They will often propose directions for further research that are suggested by the current study's findings. Sometimes the conclusions are the last few paragraphs of the discussion section without a separate heading.

References

The documents cited in the article are listed in alphabetical order by the last name of the first author of each document. Only documents that are specifically cited in the paper should appear in this reference list. Reference items are formatted according to the style of the journal in which the article appears. Journals published by the American Psychological Association (APA) (*Developmental Psychology* and *Journal of Family Psychology,* for example) use the style described in the *Publication Manual of the American Psychological Association* (American Psychological Association, 2002). Journals published by the American Sociological Association (ASA) (such as *American Sociological Review*) use a style that is similar to that of the APA and is described in the *ASA Style Guide* (American Sociological Association, 1997). Journals published or sponsored by the National Council on Family Relations (*Journal of Marriage and the Family, Journal of Family Issues,* and *Family Relations,* for example) generally use the APA style.

Tables

A good table supplements (but does not duplicate) the textual material in the body of the article. Generally, it's better to use as few tables as possible to convey the information found in the research. The tables should be organized around the primary hypotheses of the study. The titles of the tables should be clear and unambiguous; ideally, the table titles will identify the primary dependent variable and, if practical, the independent variables as well. Tables are numbered so that the author can refer to *Table 3,* for example, without having to mention the entire title.

Figures

Most journals prefer that authors keep the number of figures to a minimum (*tables,* by the way, consist only of numbers and text; *figures* contain graphics and are less precise than tables). Like tables, figures are numbered consecutively.

Where Do I Go From Here?

At this point, you've probably got a stack of articles (or maybe printouts of abstracts from an indexing system) that seem relevant to your topic. You will want to begin by skimming all the articles. At this stage, it may help to ignore the *methods* and *results* sections, and focus on the *introduction* and *discussion* sections. As you read the articles, you can begin to cull the stack a bit by deciding which articles are relevant to your topic and which are not. Eliminate the articles that you've decided aren't directly relevant to your current project, but file them in case you reconsider them later.

Now consider the articles that you've decided are relevant to your project. Read them again but this time without omitting any sections. Note any patterns or inconsistencies in the theories, methods, findings, and conclusions of the studies. Does a single theory seem to guide all these studies, or do they work within differing theoretical traditions? Do these studies tend to use the same or different methods of data collection? Are their findings in agreement, or do they conflict? How do the authors interpret these findings?

At the same time, be alert to gaps in the literature. What types of issues or variables are seldom or never addressed by the research? What populations haven't been studied? Are the studies relatively recent, or are they old? Might some body of theory be relevant that hasn't been applied to this particular problem? Often, the last few paragraphs of the discussion or conclusion section can tip you off to problems or possibilities in the literature. Authors will frequently discuss possible limitations in their own work or suggestions for future research.

You should also examine the reference lists at the end of each article. Notice which items tend to be cited by the articles you've collected; if those often-cited items aren't already in your stack of photocopies, they should be. Such often-cited or seminal papers are important for several reasons. First, if many of the current studies in your topic cite a particular paper, it must be important to the development of research in your area. Second, authors often assume that their readers are familiar with the classic or seminal works in their area; if you haven't read these papers, you may not be getting the full sense of what's going into the research. Third, these works may suggest possibilities or directions for research that, for whatever reason, no one ever pursued.

SSCI has some unusual capabilities that provide an effective way to build up a bibliography. After identifying the classic or seminal works in a particular area, you can use SSCI's "Cited Reference Search" to identify all the items in the database that cited those works. This technique often can identify articles that are relevant to your topic that might not have been uncovered through other methods.

How Do Journal Articles Get Published?

We sometimes hear about the publish-or-perish syndrome for academic researchers, but most people don't realize how difficult it is to publish an article in a major journal. The process varies somewhat across journals, but most follow a basic pattern.

First, the author or authors (most research articles have multiple authors) submit the manuscript to the journal. The journal editor then sends copies of the manuscript to two or three reviewers, usually individuals chosen for their expertise in the field. The reviewers read the manuscript and send the editor two sets of comments: one set to be sent to the author and a second for the editor's eyes only. The reviewers can critique any aspect of the paper: review of the literature, hypotheses, methods, analytic techniques, and conclusions—even the writing style.

The reviewers are especially concerned with two issues. First, is the research important enough to merit taking up valuable pages in the journal? Because of page limitations, most journals reject more than 50% of submissions, and major journals often approach 90% rejection rates.

Second, was the research conducted in such a way that the conclusions drawn by the authors are valid? Publication of an article by a major journal implies approval of the research design by the reviewers and the journal's editorial staff, so most journal editors are concerned about the quality of the research design and analytic techniques.

Once the editor has the reviewers' comments in hand, one of three decisions must be conveyed to the author. First, the editor can decide to publish the manuscript in its current form (or perhaps with minor editorial revisions). This is extremely rare, because most reviewers raise at least several major concerns that have to be dealt with in a revision. The second possible decision by the editor is to ask the author to revise and resubmit the manuscript for further review, taking into account the criticisms and suggestions of the reviewers. The revised manuscript will be reviewed again, usually by the original reviewers. The third decision the editor can make, of course, is to reject the manuscript outright. The rejection might be based on the topic's irrelevance or on fundamental flaws in the conceptualization, research design, or analytic techniques that cannot be fixed with a revision.

The time lag from submission to the editor's decision varies greatly across journals, but usually it is 6 to 12 weeks. If the author receives a revise-and-resubmit decision, the review process will take another 6 to 12 weeks (plus the time spent revising the manuscript). You can see that even under ideal circumstances, 6 to 12 months can pass between the time of the original submission of a manuscript and the editor's final acceptance of that manuscript for publication. Add about a 6-month lag between acceptance and actual appearance in print, and you have at least a year's span, if not much longer, between submission and actual publication.

This reviewing process, or **peer review,** is one of the great strengths of scientific disciplines. Most journals do blind reviews, meaning that all identifying information is removed from the manuscripts that the reviewers read.

The goal is to publish the best-conducted and most important research, regardless of who has written it.

Does this rigorous reviewing process ensure that every article published in a major journal is of uniformly high quality? Unfortunately, no. The reality is that journal editors and reviewers make mistakes. Fortunately, the public nature of the scientific enterprise permits members of the scientific community to publish critiques of the articles (known as *comments*) that point out what they believe are flaws in the original article. Two interesting examples of this self-correcting process of science are demonstrated in Trussell and Rao's (1987) criticism of White's (1987) conclusion that premarital cohabitation increases subsequent marital stability, and Peterson's (1996) critique of Weitzman's (1985) findings about the economic consequences of divorce for women.

Research Monographs

Some research on families and children is published in the form of books (usually called *research monographs*). Much greater in length, monographs allow more extensive presentations of theory and research findings than do journal articles. Research monographs also go through a review process. The reviewing of monographs is not blind because the reviewers—being experts in the field—usually are aware of who is doing research on what topics; so even if identifying material is removed from the draft of the monograph, the reviewer probably can identify the author or authors. Because of this, and because contracts for monographs are typically offered before the draft is completed, research monographs may not be as critically reviewed as an article appearing in a major journal.

Another difference between journal articles and research monographs is the time lag until publication. Several years typically elapse between the beginning of work on a research monograph and its appearance in print. As a result, if you're looking for the most current research on a particular topic, you will probably want to begin by searching the indices (such as *Sociological Abstracts* and *PsycINFO*) to produce a list of recent journal articles, then move on to the research monographs on that topic.

Other Types of Publications

Although primarily published as journal articles or research monographs, research on children and families also appears in other forms as well. Each year, the professional organizations of scholars that study families and children (for example, the National Council on Family Relations, the ASA, and the APA) hold national conferences at which hundreds of conference papers are presented. Many of these eventually appear in professional journals, but some do not. Because most of these papers do not go through an elaborate peer-review process, their status in the scientific world is somewhat less than that of published articles. Moreover, these papers haven't appeared in print, making them somewhat difficult to obtain. The major indices, such as *Sociological Abstracts* and *PsycINFO,* will have entries for most of these papers, along with instructions on how to obtain copies.

Doctoral dissertations and master's theses are another source of research on families. *Sociological Abstracts* and *PsycINFO* index dissertations completed at U.S. universities; *Dissertation Abstracts International* also provides listings and abstracts of dissertations and information on obtaining copies of the dissertations themselves.

Government agencies such as the Department of Health and Human Services, the National Institutes of Health, and the U.S. Census Bureau as well as private foundations and organizations such as the Children's Defense Fund, the David and Lucille Packard Foundation, and others publish agency reports of research funded by their organizations. The reports themselves are not usually peer reviewed, but they often appear in journal articles or research monographs. Searches of the World Wide Web (discussed in Chapter 4) are apt to turn up such reports.

Unpublished manuscripts are the most difficult documents to locate and obtain. These are usually works in progress that researchers have circulated before submission for publication or presentation at a conference. Because they have not been reviewed, one must be cautious in how much credence to lend to their findings. As a general rule, you should try to avoid citing unpublished materials unless it is essential.

Study Questions

1. Choose a research topic (for example, child abuse, economic consequences of divorce for women, or elder care). Learn how to use *Sociological Abstracts,* SSCI or *PsycINFO* at your local library or over the Internet, and conduct a search on your topic. List five articles that you find that are relevant to your topic.

2. Choose a well-known family researcher and use the index system of your choice to find articles published by that person over the last 10 years.

3. Find an article in a major family research journal such as *Journal of Marriage and the Family* or *Journal of Family Issues.* Compare the structure of the article to that in this chapter. What sections are missing? Are there any key pieces of information absent from the article?

4. Pick any one of the journal articles listed below in the For Further Reading section and report how many times it was cited in the literature last year.

For Further Reading

American Psychological Association. (2002). *Publication manual of the American Psychological Association* (5th ed.). Washington, DC: American Psychological Association.

American Sociological Association. (1997). *American Sociological Association style guide* (2nd ed.). Washington, DC: American Sociological Association.

Greenstein, T. N. (1990). Marital disruption and the employment of married women. *Journal of Marriage and Family, 52,* 657–676.

Peterson, R. R. (1996). A re-evaluation of the economic consequences of divorce. *American Sociological Review, 61,* 528–536.

Sanchez, L. (1994). Gender, labor allocations, and the psychology of entitlement within the home. *Social Forces, 73,* 533–553.

Trussell, J., & Rao, K. V. (1987). Premarital cohabitation and marital stability: A reassessment of the Canadian evidence. *Journal of Marriage and the Family, 51,* 535–540.

Weitzman, L. J. (1985). *The divorce revolution: The unexpected social and economic consequences for women and children in America.* New York: Free Press.

White, J. M. (1987). Premarital cohabitation and marital stability in Canada. *Journal of Marriage and the Family, 49,* 641–647.

4

Using the Internet to Study Families

The Internet is an international network consisting of thousands of interconnected computers and computer networks. It was created in 1969 by research funded by the U.S. Department of Defense through its Advanced Research Projects Agency (ARPA), which gave the Internet its original name—ARPANET. Despite its military origins, civilian researchers heavily used ARPANET; by 1983, it was reserved for civilian use, and MILNET was created for military applications. The combination of these two networks came to be known as the Internet.

The incredible growth of the Internet surprised nearly every industry expert. The National Telecommunications and Information Administration (1999) reported that the Internet passed 50 million users in its first four years. By contrast, radio took 38 years and television 13 years to gain an audience of 50 million people. Some surveys suggest that nearly half of all respondents see the Internet as their primary source of news about current events.

The two best-known aspects of the Internet are the World Wide Web (WWW or the Web) and electronic mail (e-mail). The Web allows computer users anywhere in the world to access any other computer that is connected to the Web. The Web contains a wealth of information about research and organizations involved with families. E-mail provides a cheap, fast, and reliable alternative to conventional *snail mail*.

Two other important aspects of the Web are similar systems that allow groups of like-minded users to communicate as a newsgroup (Usenet) or through a mailing list (Listserv). Users worldwide can post and read messages on these systems, which are organized around topics of interest (for example, medicine, investments, sports, and so forth). They are widely used by academics and practitioners who study families and children. Finally, the development of electronic journals holds the promise of reducing costs and facilitating the dissemination of scientific research.

Web Sites of Interest to Family Researchers

Hundreds of organizations interested in families have created sites on the Web. All the major professional organizations for family researchers, teachers, and practitioners have Web sites. The National Council of Family Relations has a site at www.ncfr.org. The American Sociological Association is at www.asanet.org; its Family Section is located at www.asanet.org/sectionfamily, and its section on Sociology of Children is at www.asanet.org/section/children.html. The American Psychological Association's (APA's) Web site is www.apa.org; and its Children, Youth, and Families office site is www.apa.org/pi/cyf. The National Association of Social Workers can be found at www.naswdc.org, the American Association for Marriage and

Family Therapy is at www.aamft.org, and the American Association for Family and Consumer Sciences is located at www.aafcs.org. The National Association for the Education of Young Children can be found at www.naeyc .org, and the Council on Contemporary Families maintains a Web site at www.contemporaryfamilies.org.

Many federal government agencies are involved with families and children. A particularly useful site is the Cooperative Extension Service's National Network for Childcare at www.nncc.org. Among its useful offerings are links to hundreds of organizations interested in children and families. Some of the federal agencies that fund research and programs on families and related topics include the National Science Foundation's Directorate for Social, Behavioral, and Economic Sciences (www.nsf.gov/sbe); the National Institute of Child Health and Human Development (www.nichd.nih.gov); the National Institute on Aging (www.nih.gov/nia); and the U.S. Department of Agriculture's Cooperative State Research, Education and Extension Service (www .csrees.usda.gov).

Many foundations support research and programs involving families, such as the Annie E. Casey Foundation (www.aecf.org), which sponsors the online KIDS COUNT database (www.aecf.org/kidscount/kc2000); the Ford Foundation (www.fordfound.org); the Russell Sage Foundation (www .russellsage.org); the Robert Wood Johnson Foundation (www.rwjf.org); the Children, Families and Communities program of the David and Lucille Packard Foundation (www.packfound.org/html/children__families__and_commun .html); and the Program on Human and Community Development of the John D. and Catherine T. MacArthur Foundation (www.macfound.org/programs/ hcd/overview.htm), to name just a few. A comprehensive list of charitable foundations can be found at The Foundation Center (fdncenter.org).

Finally, many advocacy groups have Web sites. A small sampling of these includes Children Now (www.childrennow.org), the Children's Defense Fund (www.childrensdefense.org), ZERO TO THREE (www.zerotothree.org), Focus on the Family (family.org), the National Center for Fathering (www .fathers.com), the Family Research Council (www.frc.org), and the Institute for American Values (www.Americanvalues.org). Some of these groups are political in nature, and it is wise to cast a critical eye on their claims and research results.

Search Engines

One of the great benefits of the Web is the ability to locate information quickly and easily. What used to take hours of research at the local library, and often required a phone call to find the right person at the right office, can now be done in a matter of minutes on the Web. To make it easier to find information, on the Web we typically use a **search engine.**

A search engine is a site on the Web that searches for sites containing words or phrases that you specify. The different types of search engines all work in pretty much the same way. Most search engines take one or more keywords entered by the user, search the contents of every Web page stored in their databases (or only pages in selected categories if desired), and display the results. In most cases, the resulting pages are given a score (determined by the number of times the search criteria are met in each page), and ordered from the highest score (best match) to the lowest. Some of the most commonly used search engines are Yahoo (www.yahoo.com) and Google (www.google.com). Another useful search engine is FedStats (www.fedstats.gov), which searches the Web sites of more than 70 government agencies for information.

For example, to find statistics on teenage pregnancy, using FedStats, I entered *teenage* and *pregnancy* as the search terms. The search engine returned a list of 43 documents, one of which was a recent press release from the Department of Health and Human Services outlining data on teenage pregnancy and a link to a full-text report on the subject.

Some search engines reduce your workload by searching several other search engines simultaneously. MetaCrawler (www.metacrawler.com) is a *metasearch engine.* By the time you read this, even more powerful methods to search the Web will probably have appeared.

What Are Mailing Lists?

The most common form of electronic mailing list on the Internet is known as Listserv® (Listserv is a registered trademark of the L-Soft Corporation). Listserv is a system that allows nearly anyone to create, manage, and control electronic mailing lists on the Internet. To glimpse how ubiquitous these lists have become, consider that as of April 1999, through more than 162,000 registered lists with nearly 60 million subscribers, more than 20 million e-mail messages were sent per day.

As with real-world distribution lists, electronic mailing lists make it possible for people to confer in a painless manner by way of the written word. The e-mail software simply replaces the copying machine with its associated costs, delays, and frustrations. In fact, e-mail lists are easier to use than most modern copiers, and a lot less likely to jam at just the worst possible moment. Because e-mail is delivered in a matter of minutes, e-mailing lists can do a lot more than merely supplement the traditional paper distribution lists.

Researchers and academics have embraced Listserv, creating dozens of specialized mailing lists. Of particular interest to students of families and children are the Family Science Network (FAMLYSCI) and FAMNET, which is organized by the American Sociological Association's Section on Family. These and similar Listservs connect thousands of scholars, researchers, and practitioners worldwide with an interest in families and children.

To participate in Listserv discussions, you need to subscribe to the list. Typically, this is accomplished by sending e-mail to the Listserv (you will need to know the e-mail address of the particular list you wish to join). This e-mail message should have only one line of text:

```
subscribe <name> <your name>;
```

<name> is the name of the Listserv, and <your name> should be your full name (e.g., John Smith) and not a nickname. Once you have subscribed to the Listserv, you can ask questions or participate in the discussions by sending e-mail to the list. Be sure to provide a descriptive subject line (e.g., "Question About Divorce Statistics"). Every time a subscriber sends a message to the list, all other subscribers get an e-mail copy of that message. Some lists allow the use of the digest option, in which each day's messages are put together in a single e-mail message sent once daily.

Sometimes finding mailing lists on a topic of interest can be difficult. And some lists are open only to members of particular organizations or individuals with specific qualifications; such lists don't generally advertise their existence. If you know of any Web sites devoted to the topic you are looking for, check those pages to see if a mailing list is mentioned. You can also ask other people who are interested in that topic if they know of any mailing lists. Several organizations post lists of mailing lists on the Web. You can also try doing a Web search using the topics of interest to see if a mailing list turns up.

What Are Newsgroups?

Usenet is an international network of newsgroups. A **newsgroup** is a discussion forum organized around a specific topic. An estimated 20 million people regularly participate in thousands of newsgroups devoted to almost every topic imaginable. Each user is free to post, read, and reply to messages from all other users. As such, newsgroups serve two key functions. First, they are an important information resource. No matter how obscure your question might be, a newsgroup on the Web is probably related to it. Second, newsgroups also perform a news function. Information about current events travels quickly on the Web, even when conventional media are unable or unwilling to broadcast a particular story.

You've probably noticed that newsgroups sound a lot like mailing lists; indeed they are similar. Two important differences exist, however. One significant difference is that usually only mailing list subscribers have access to the messages posted on the list; you can't just *lurk* on a mailing list. Newsgroup messages, however, can be easily read by anyone with newsreader software (which is generally available as freeware). Most newsreader programs offer the option of listing all the newsgroups available on your system.

The other major difference between newsgroups and mailing lists is how the users receive the messages. In mailing lists, the messages are transmitted directly to each subscriber in the form of e-mail messages. Some of the more active mailing lists can produce dozens of such messages each day, and subscribers have to handle each incoming message with their e-mail software or choose the digest option. With a newsgroup, you can use your newsreader to browse a list of the subject lines of messages that have been posted about each topic, and then you can open and read only the ones you find interesting.

What Are Electronic Journals?

The **electronic journal** appeared in response to both the high cost of conventionally produced journals and as an assertion of intellectual freedom. Dozens of electronic journals are now available to the academic community. All indications are that these publications are likely to proliferate in the future. Access arrangements vary, as do the types of services offered; you may be asked to register for certain publications. Users are well-advised to read introductory information closely. Some of the journals are electronic versions of hardcopy publications, and others are special electronic editions that are not necessarily the equivalent of hardcopy journals. Some electronic journals subject submitted manuscripts to a full review process, but others do not.

The Internet as a Source of Data

In Chapter 6, I discuss using the Internet to collect survey data. The Internet can serve as a source of data for research on families in other ways, as well.

For example, the Federal Interagency Forum on Child and Family Statistics has a site at www.childstats.gov. Its Web page provides links to many different types of data on children and families from federal agencies. Most of the major data-collection series (such as the Current Population Survey and the General Social Survey) maintain Web sites and are discussed in Chapter 12.

Much census and related data are now available for access at the U.S. Census Bureau's DataFerrett system (www.dataferrett.census.gov). DataFerrett can access the Current Population Surveys, the American Housing Surveys, the Consumer Expenditure Surveys, and the Survey of Income and Program Participation. The Integrated Public Use Microdata Series (www.ipums.umn.edu) at the University of Minnesota creates customized extracts of census data going as far back as the 1850 Census.

For background information and summary tables, most of the *Statistical Abstract of the United States* is available online at www.census.gov/statab/www. Many state agencies also make their information available over the Internet. The United Nations makes much of its data available through its Web site at www.un.org.

Advantages and Disadvantages of the Internet for Family Research

The Internet provides great opportunities for students of the family. Using electronic mailing lists or newsgroups, we can keep abreast of breaking developments in the field, often months before articles or books are available in print form. We can *broadcast* requests for help or suggestions on family-related topics. Most of the family-related organizations now have Web sites with helpful links. Using e-mail, we can communicate with authors and researchers to find out about projects or ask questions about published research.

The Internet has a dark side as well. As most Internet users are aware, Web content is subjected to negligible quality control. Anyone can create a Web site and post whatever they please without regard to the information's accuracy. Often, advocacy groups of one kind or another will create Web sites to support their own agendas, and separating factual (or even meaningful) information from rhetoric and downright deception can be difficult. Because many sites are relatively short lived, citing a Web site address can sometimes create problems in a manuscript. By the time the manuscript appears in print, the Web site may have changed addresses or disappeared completely. For further information about using the Internet, you may wish to consult Jones (1999) or Mann and Stewart (2000).

Study Questions

1. Use the Internet to obtain the number of married-couple households in the United States for the most recent year available.

2. Go to the Web site of the family-related professional organization of your choice and find out when and where their next annual conference will be held.

3. Choose some family-related topic of interest to you (for example, father's rights, abortion, or cohabitation) and locate opposing viewpoints from two different advocacy groups on the Web. Evaluate each viewpoint.

For Further Reading

Jones, S. (1999). *Doing Internet research*. Thousand Oaks, CA: Sage.

Mann, C., & Stewart, F. (2000). *Internet communication and qualitative research: A handbook for researching online*. Thousand Oaks, CA: Sage.

National Telecommunications and Information Administration. (1999). *Falling through the net: Defining the digital divide*. Washington, DC: Government Printing Office.

5

How Do We Measure Concepts?

S ocial researchers are faced with something of a dilemma when they attempt to measure concepts. Take, for example, a concept such as marital satisfaction. This concept is abstract; you cannot touch, feel, or see marital satisfaction. Yet, we somehow have to translate this abstraction into some kind of concrete **measurement**. We have to figure out a way to get people to tell us, as accurately as possible, how satisfied they are with their marriages.

Much of our thinking about families and children begins with what Babbie (2004) calls *conceptions*. We each have a conception of what defines marital satisfaction. But it's clear that marital satisfaction is not a physical object or quantity that can be readily observed and measured. How do we translate the relatively abstract and unobservable concept of marital satisfaction into something that we can measure and study?

Kaplan (1964) suggested three types of things that can be measured. A **direct observable** is a physical characteristic that can be observed directly, such as the number of people present at a meeting. A person's response to a questionnaire item about the number of people in a household is an **indirect observable**—an indirect representation of a characteristic or object. A **construct** is a creation based on observation, but it cannot be observed directly or indirectly. Marital satisfaction is an example of a construct. We may be able to observe consequences of marital satisfaction (e.g., marital stability), and we may be able to observe causes or antecedents of marital satisfaction (e.g., an equitable division of household labor between husband and wife); but we cannot observe marital satisfaction itself.

Operationalization is the name given to this process of translating abstractions into concrete measurement processes. In this process, we need to make a number of decisions about how to translate an abstract construct, such as marital satisfaction, so we can measure the marital satisfaction of our selected respondents.

Characteristics of a Good Measurement Procedure

In Chapter 2, I distinguished between variables and their states, levels, or attributes. Gender is a variable; female is an attribute of gender. Income is a variable; $45,000 is a state or level of income. One important decision to make in the operationalization process is what and how many attributes, states, or levels a variable will have in the measurement process.

A good measurement procedure is characterized by three key qualities. First, the set of attributes representing a variable must be exhaustive and inclusive. That is, all possible responses or states must be represented by a state, level, or attribute of the variable. If we were operationalizing the variable marital status, we would find that using only the categories *married* and *single* would produce many blank stares from our respondents. We would probably need to include *never married, divorced but not remarried, married but separated,* and *widowed* as well.

Our second concern is that the attributes, states, or levels chosen to represent a variable must be mutually exclusive. No respondent should be able to be placed in more than one category. In the five-category scheme to measure marital status (never married, currently married, married but separated, divorced but not remarried, and widowed), no person could meaningfully claim to fall in more than one category.

Finally, we need to be concerned with our attribute scheme's precision. Ideally, our category scheme should use more, rather than fewer, distinctions when feasible. For example, rather than coding certain respondents as Protestant, it is probably more useful to include the choices Baptist, Episcopalian, Methodist, and so on. In this way you can determine how many respondents are of each denomination. But if you fail to allow respondents to describe whether they're Baptist, Episcopalian, or Methodist, you will never know.

Levels of Measurement

These three qualities of measurement processes—inclusive and exhaustive, mutually exclusive, and precise—are important to consider for all variables. The variables themselves, however, may be measured in vastly different ways. **Level of measurement** refers to the properties that define the measurement process itself. Most social and behavioral data are measured at one of four levels of measurement: nominal, ordinal, interval, or ratio.

Levels of Measurement: Nominal

Some variables have attributes that meet only the minimal requirements of being exhaustive and mutually exclusive. Some examples of nominal variables are religion, race, gender, city of residence, and marital status. Each of these variables, when properly defined, has a set of logically exhaustive and mutually exclusive categories or attributes. In other words, nominal variables identify the attributes associated with a variable without making any statements about whether one state or level is more or less than any other state or level. With variables measured at the nominal level, it's not possible to rank categories along any particular dimension, nor is it possible to state with great precision how much of the attribute is present.

It's also important to note that for nominally scaled variables, the differences between categories are not mathematically meaningful. For example, let's say that we gave the following response choices to the question "What is your current marital status?"

1. Currently married

2. Married, but separated

3. Divorced, not remarried

4. Widowed

5. Never married

The fact that we assigned the number 5 to the response "never married" doesn't mean that it's one point better than "widowed" or five times as much as "currently married." For variables scaled at the nominal level, only the categories are meaningful—not the distances or gaps between categories or the numerical values we arbitrarily assign to the categories for coding purposes.

Levels of Measurement: Ordinal

Variables that are scaled at the **ordinal level of measurement** have all the properties of nominally scaled variables, but they add an important characteristic: The categories are ranked or ordered along some evaluative dimension. That is, unlike nominally scaled variables, ordinally scaled variables are assumed to represent some underlying continuum (e.g., from least to most or least desirable to most desirable). Some examples of variables that are typically measured at the ordinal level are social class (working class, middle class, upper class), marital happiness (not very happy, somewhat happy, very happy), or highest degree obtained (less than high school, high school diploma, college degree, graduate or professional degree).

Another type of measure that is often considered at the ordinal level is a **Likert scale** item (discussed further in Chapter 9). For example, we might ask respondents to indicate how they feel about this statement: "If a husband and wife both work full-time, they should share housework tasks equally." Do you

1. Strongly disagree

2. Disagree somewhat

3. Undecided, not sure

4. Agree somewhat

5. Strongly agree

Notice that such a variable has an exhaustive and mutually exclusive set of categories and that the categories clearly are ranked or ordered along the dimension of agreeing with the idea of sharing the housework. Those who say they "agree somewhat" with the statement are more strongly supportive of husbands and wives sharing housework than someone who says they "disagree somewhat." However, we can't say how much more supportive these people are, and we undoubtedly can't say that someone who agrees somewhat is twice as supportive of husbands and wives sharing housework as someone who disagrees somewhat. For ordinally scaled variables, the differences between categories are not mathematically meaningful because the numbers we assign to the categories merely reflect the ordering of the response choices.

One advantage of ordinal measurement is that people can often make comparative judgments relatively easily, whereas making an absolute judgment is far more difficult. For example, although respondents could probably tell us which aspect of their family lives gave them the most satisfaction, they would be hard pressed to tell us exactly how much more satisfaction they got from their family leisure time than from doing housework chores.

Levels of Measurement: Interval

Besides including all the characteristics of nominal and ordinal variables, variables that are measured at the **interval level** have differences between scale units that are meaningful and constant. Probably the most commonly used interval level measures employed in the social sciences are standardized intelligence tests. The scale is designed so that the 10-point difference between an intelligence quotient (IQ) score of 120 and one of 110 has the same meaning as the 10-point difference between scores of 140 and 130 (or, for that matter, any 10-point difference anywhere along the scale).

Although, strictly speaking, Likert-style items don't meet the requirements for interval-level measurement, they are often treated as if they do. Methodologists and statisticians don't seem to agree on whether this type of treatment is appropriate. One way to circumvent this criticism is to combine a number of Likert-style items into a composite index of some construct, and treat the scale total as an interval-level measure. There is more on this in Chapter 10.

Levels of Measurement: Ratio

Variables that are measured at the **ratio level of measurement** include all the characteristics of nominal, ordinal, and interval variables. What distinguishes the ratio level of measurement from the other levels is that the scale of measurement has a theoretically defined origin, or zero point. Income in dollars is a ratio-level measure, because zero dollars means the absence of money. Number of children in a family is a ratio-level measure because zero children indicates the absence of children in the family. For comparison, note that temperature in kelvins is a ratio-level measure (because the zero point is theoretically defined as the absence of all molecular motion), but temperature in degrees Fahrenheit is not a ratio-level measure (because 0°F is an arbitrary point on the scale).

For ratio variables, as for interval variables, the scale intervals mean the same thing at all points on the scale (e.g., a $1 increase in income means the same at all points along the income continuum). For ratio variables, however, it also makes mathematical sense to compare different levels in a multiplicative sense. For example, a family with four children has twice as many children as one with two children; someone who earns $50,000 has twice as much income as someone who earns $25,000. But although 200 kelvins is twice as warm as 100 kelvins, an 80°F day is not twice as warm as a 40°F day.

Summary of Levels of Measurement

It may have occurred to you that the same concept might be measured at several different levels of measurement. Marital satisfaction, for example, can be measured at the nominal level by asking respondents, "Are you satisfied with your marriage?" and offering response choices of "Yes, I am satisfied with my marriage" and "No, I am not satisfied with my marriage." Marital satisfaction can be measured at the ordinal level by asking, "How satisfied are you with your marriage?" and offering choices of "very dissatisfied," "somewhat dissatisfied," "unsure," "somewhat satisfied," and "very satisfied." Similarly, family size might be measured at the ordinal level by classifying families as small, medium, and large or at the ratio level by finding out exactly how many members there are in a given family.

A key reason that level of measurement is so important is that different statistical techniques require measurement at particular levels. Some procedures, for example, are only appropriate for interval- or ratio-level data. Other techniques are appropriate for both nominal- and ordinal-level data, but some are specific to ordinal-level data. Whichever level of measurement is used, however, the key issues in data quality are reliability and validity.

What Are Reliability and Validity?

No measurement procedure is perfect. In statistical terms, no measurement procedure is error free. We know that some respondents will provide incorrect responses because they don't know the answer to our question. Others will deliberately give wrong answers to appear more socially acceptable or answer the questions in the way they think the researcher wants them answered. Still other respondents will be confused by the phrasing or content of the question and answer incorrectly. Some respondents will give different answers to our questions at different times.

Social scientists gauge the amount of error in measurement in terms of reliability and validity. **Reliability** refers to the stability or consistency of a measurement operation. **Validity** refers to whether we're really measuring the concept that we intended to measure. More detailed discussions of each follow.

Reliability

If a measurement is really a good way of operationalizing a construct, that measurement procedure should yield the same result each time it is used (assuming, of course, that the value of the underlying construct hasn't changed over time). We refer to this type of reliability as **stability.** Another type of reliability deals with whether different observers using the same measurement procedure come up with the same result. This second type of reliability is known as **consistency.**

Stability

In the National Longitudinal Survey of Youth (NLSY), a sample of men and women were asked a series of questions about their work, education, and lives in general. In two separate interviews in 1983 and 1984, women were asked, "At what age did you first have sexual intercourse?" Obviously, a woman's age at first intercourse can't change over time. The response from any particular woman should not change from year to year if the measure is perfectly reliable.

If this measure were perfectly reliable, we would expect to get exactly the same response from each woman at each interview. Typically, however, some responses do change over time. Of the 5,788 women responding to this question at both interviews, only 57% gave the same response both times! Yet, of the women who gave different responses, nearly all (90%) gave a response in 1984 that was within two years of their 1983 response.

So, is this measure reliable or not? One way to think about this issue is to look at the difference between the average age given for first sexual intercourse at the 1983 response and compare it to the 1984 average. Overall, the average difference between the two responses is 0.03 year (about 11 days!). On that basis, we can conclude that the measure has very good reliability. Another way of looking at the reliability of this measure is to think in statistical terms. If this measure were perfectly reliable, the correlation coefficient (a numerical index of similarity) between the 1983 and 1984 responses would be equal to 1.0. For these data, the correlation is about 0.97, suggesting high reliability in the sense of stability.

Consistency

Another way of thinking about reliability is in terms of consistency. Whereas stability refers to the reliability of a measure over time, consistency refers to its reliability across observers or across items. Reliability in the first sense is known as **interobserver reliability,** or agreement; reliability across items is known as **internal consistency,** or internal reliability. In Chapter 9, I discuss the issue of internal reliability in the context of index construction.

If we were doing a study of marital quality, we might have 6 family therapists observe 10 married couples discussing their marriages. We then ask each counselor to rate the quality of each couple's marriage on a scale of 1 (very poor) to 10 (very good). We would expect that if all 6 therapists are using the same criteria to judge the quality of the marriages, they would have a high degree of agreement. If the counselors agree on the marital quality for each couple, the measure of marital quality has reliability in the sense of consistency. We could even calculate an index of agreement where 0 equals no agreement whatsoever between the 6 therapists and 1.0 equals perfect agreement. Of course, just because 6 marriage counselors agree on how happy the couples are doesn't mean that their estimates are meaningful or valid.

Validity

In its truest sense, validity refers to how well we're measuring some underlying construct. Are we measuring what we think that we're measuring? The ideal way to measure the validity of a measurement operation is to compare the results of the measurement to the actual (real) value of the construct. Unfortunately, this usually isn't possible, because for most of the constructs we want to measure, actual value can't be determined. How can you learn a person's real attitude toward abortion? How could you know the real level of a person's marital satisfaction?

Consequently, most of our measures are indirect. We rely, for example, on a person's response to our questions about abortion to determine how that person feels about the abortion issue. When we attempt to get an indication of the real value of the construct, we are aware that our measurement process may be imperfect. Methodologists call a person's real attitude about abortion rights the *true* score; responses to our questions about abortion rights are the *observed* score. Every observed score is the sum of two parts: the true score plus an error component.

The difference between the true score and the observed score is known as **measurement error.** Some of this error may be **random measurement error:** It is unrelated to the real value being measured. These random errors tend to cancel each other out and won't bias a measurement in any particular direction.

More serious for social and behavioral researchers is **systematic measurement error,** which can bias the result of the measurement process in one direction or another. For example, in a survey of parenting strategies, we might ask parents how many times in the past month they have had to physically punish their children. We expect to find that the responses are going to be biased downward—that is, we expect that parents systematically underreport the use of physical punishment—because many parents feel that use of physical punishment is indicative of a bad parent (even if they themselves use physical punishment). Moreover, parents who frequently use physical punishment are more likely to underreport such activity than those who rarely use physical punishment. Similarly, responses to a question on marital happiness might be systematically biased upward, because people often aren't willing to admit that they are unhappy with their marriages. In other words, the measurement error on these measures is probably not random. Singleton and Straits (2004) present a clear discussion of measurement error in the more general context of reliability and validity.

To deal with these problems, social scientists have developed a number of alternate indicators of a measure's validity.

Face Validity

When we talk about **face validity,** we mean whether the instrument looks like it's measuring what it's supposed to be measuring. A measure of marital satisfaction should not contain items about the legalization of marijuana or attitudes about gun control.

Of course, just because a measure of marital satisfaction contains items that *look like* they're measuring marital satisfaction doesn't necessarily mean that the instrument is measuring what it's supposed to be measuring. For example, we might ask a sample of married persons, "How satisfied are you with your marriage?" with response categories "not very satisfied," "somewhat satisfied," and "very satisfied." Such a measure looks valid from a face validity standpoint; clearly, the question is about marital satisfaction, and the response choices seem to capture the range of possible satisfaction levels. However, the item might have questionable validity if people tend to overreport their actual levels of marital satisfaction.

Criterion Validity

Criterion validity deals with how well a measure correlates with (or predicts) external criteria, including behaviors. There are two major forms of criterion validity. **Predictive validity** reflects the ability of a measure to predict future behaviors or conditions. We could expect our measure of marital satisfaction to correlate highly with how many violent arguments the couple had in the last 12 months. After all, you could assume that if a couple has violent arguments, they are not too satisfied with their marriage. Similarly, you would expect a valid measure of marital satisfaction to predict with some accuracy which couples would most likely divorce over the next five years.

Criterion validity can also reflect how well a measure correlates with alternative measures of the same phenomenon taken at approximately the same point of time; this type of criterion validity is known as **concurrent validity**. A new measure of spousal communication skills, for example, should correlate well with existing measures of such skills, especially those known to be well validated.

Construct Validity

Construct validity refers to how well a measure correlates with other theoretical constructs. We can expect a measure of marital satisfaction to correlate well with measures of such constructs as marital happiness, affection for one's spouse, and perceptions of fairness of the division of household tasks. If the measure of marital satisfaction did not correlate well with such measures, we would be suspicious that maybe it wasn't really measuring marital satisfaction.

Some writers argue that predictive or criterion validity is the most important indicator of a measure's overall validity. When measures of external criteria such as behavior are unavailable, however, construct validity can be a useful indication of how well we're measuring our concept.

Content Validity

Marital satisfaction probably has many different aspects or dimensions. Married persons might be satisfied or dissatisfied with their sex lives, how much work they have to do around the house, how much free time they have, how their paid work relates to their family life, how well they communicate with their spouses, and other dimensions as well. **Content validity** refers to how well the measure taps the full range of dimensions or meanings of the underlying construct.

Some Thoughts on Reliability and Validity

Imagine four different clocks. One of them is broken and always reads six o'clock. Another clock works perfectly but is set exactly 2 minutes ahead of the actual time. A third clock is fast and gains 1 minute every hour. The fourth clock keeps perfect time and is set correctly. Obviously, the fourth clock is both perfectly reliable and perfectly valid. But what about the other clocks?

The broken clock is perfectly reliable. No matter how many times we look at it, it always says the same time: six o'clock. What about the validity of this clock? The clock is exactly right—it is a perfectly valid measure of the current time—twice a day (at six o'clock in the morning and again at six o'clock at night). In fact, if we took our measurements at six o'clock each day, we might conclude that it is perfectly valid. Overall, however, this clock is not a valid measure of the current time, because it is correct only twice in each 24-hour period.

The second clock—the one that is always 2 minutes fast—is also perfectly reliable. If we check the clock each day at six o'clock, it will always read 6:02. As far as validity is concerned, this clock will never have the correct time, but it is an excellent indicator of the correct time.

The clock that gains 1 minute every hour is unreliable. If we check it at six o'clock each day, the clock's reading could be almost anything. Occasionally, this clock would have the correct time, but most of the time it's wrong.

The moral of this story is straightforward. A measure that is perfectly reliable is not necessarily perfectly valid. Yet, a measure that is perfectly valid is perfectly reliable; a measure that always gives the correct answer must always give the same answer (assuming that the underlying construct hasn't changed).

Sometimes a measure that we know is not perfectly valid may nonetheless be useful. None of our measures in the social and behavioral sciences are perfectly valid, but they don't have to be perfect to be of some value to us. Think about that the next time someone is critical of opinion poll results—while the numbers aren't perfect, they are probably a pretty good indication of how people feel.

Finally, keep in mind that the time to have these concerns about reliability and validity is before the instrument is constructed and before the data are collected. Once you've collected your data, it's too late to amend the research protocol. Whenever possible, it is important to assess the reliability and validity of the measures in our research *before* gathering our data. This may necessitate pilot studies or pretests where we gather a small amount of data and evaluate the reliability and validity of our measures before the full-scale data collection begins. It can be invaluable to simply ask someone not connected with the research to read over the questionnaire or other instruments and make some general comments.

Study Questions

1. Give four examples of family-related variables measured at each of the four levels of measurement.

2. Select an article from a recent family journal (e.g., *Journal of Marriage and the Family, Journal of Family Issues,* or *Child Development*) and identify three of the major variables in the study. Then, for each variable, identify the level of measurement used in the study.

3. Using the same article you selected above, for each variable, discuss the reliability and validity concerns raised by the authors. If the authors don't make any statements about reliability and/or validity, make sure that you report this.

For Further Reading

Babbie, E. (2004). *The practice of social research* (10th ed.). Belmont, CA: Wadsworth.

Kaplan, A. (1964). *The conduct of inquiry: Methodology for behavioral science.* San Francisco: Chandler.

Singleton, R., & Straits, B. C. (2004). *Approaches to social research* (4th ed.). New York: Oxford University Press.

6

Studying Families: Quantitative Methods

After the variables of interest have been identified, the literature has been reviewed, and a research question or a hypothesis has been presented, the questions become: How will the data necessary to study this problem be obtained? What technique of data collection should be used?

One way to think about research methods is to imagine trying to listen to a distant radio station. Many factors make it hard to follow the broadcast: background noise, static, or maybe another station transmitting on the same frequency. You need to separate the signal from the noise. Just as a good radio receiver will allow you to pick out that weak radio station from the background noise, a good research design helps assess the true effect of some independent variable (or variables) on the dependent variable (or variables). Poorly executed research designs don't reduce the amount of background noise, making it difficult to draw any meaningful inferences from the data; the effect is lost in the noise created by extraneous factors. A good research design, however, will make it possible to separate the signal from the noise and determine any effect the independent variables are having on the dependent variable.

Researchers studying families and children have a wide assortment of research strategies from which to draw. It is essential to choose the right research strategy for the topic at hand. After I review the available research strategies in this chapter and Chapter 7, I return to the issue of how to select the best strategy for a particular research topic. Each of the quantitative strategies reviewed in this chapter—experiments, survey methods, observation, and nonreactive techniques—has both advantages and disadvantages to the researcher and to the topic being studied.

Studying Families Through Experiments

The idea of an experiment conjures up images of a psychologist doing laboratory research. Whereas experimental designs are relatively uncommon in family research, the basic logic of experimentation guides our decisions in other types of research strategies. Knowing something about the logic and design of experimentation can be useful even when using other research strategies.

In most experiments, the independent variable is manipulated—changed or modified by the researcher—to observe the effects on the dependent variable. In experimental design, the independent variable is often referred to as the **manipulation** or **treatment.** When we think of experiments, we're usually thinking of what are known as **laboratory experiments.** This kind of experiment is usually conducted under highly controlled conditions. The ability to create precisely those conditions necessary to test a theory's predictions makes laboratory experiments especially valuable in testing formal theoretical models.

Bridges and Orza (1993) presented a good example of a laboratory experiment with their study of college students' evaluations of mothers differing in employment patterns following childbirth. Students received a written description of a hypothetical married mother and randomly were informed that the mother (a) was continuously employed (resumed full-time employment following a six-week maternity leave), (b) interrupted her employment (remained out of the labor force until her child was in the first grade), or (c) discontinued her employment at the time of the child's birth. The students were then asked to indicate how favorably they evaluated the mother. The independent variable here—the manipulation—is the employment status of the mother, whereas the evaluation of the mother is the dependent variable or outcome. The students reported a less favorable evaluation of the continuously employed mother than either the mother who interrupted her employment or the mother who discontinued her employment.

Another type of experiment is the **field experiment,** which is often conducted as part of a social or educational program. Field experimentation combines elements of laboratory experiments and observational research in natural settings. Three major advantages typify field experiments. First, they allow for the modification of the existing real-world environment suitable for testing a theory. Second, field experiments use the existing environment to disguise or conceal the nature or existence of the experiment. Finally, field experiments may be used either to test a theory in a natural setting or to apply a technique suggested by a theory, perhaps in laboratory research. Another common use of field experiments is to evaluate the effectiveness of an innovative program. Researchers studying the effectiveness of a domestic-violence deterrence program might design a field experiment to compare domestic-violence rates in areas using the new program to comparable rates in areas under the existing program.

One well-known example of a field experiment in the study of families is the Seattle and Denver Income Maintenance Experiment (Hannan, Tuma, & Groeneveld, 1978). In this project, approximately 5,000 low-income families were randomly assigned to one of four experimental conditions: three different levels of financial support plus one control condition in which no financial support was provided. Some of the literature suggests that such income-support programs should make single mothers more attractive as potential spouses, and consequently should affect the rate at which single women in the program would marry, but no such effect was noted in the experiment. Another body of literature suggests that such income-maintenance programs might have negative effects on marital stability—that is, married couples who receive income subsidies will be more likely to dissolve their marriages. Overall, income maintenance did tend to increase the rate of marital dissolution.

The design of experiments—whether conducted in the laboratory under highly controlled conditions or in natural settings—is guided by consideration of **threats to validity**. This concept was introduced by Campbell and Stanley (1963) and elaborated on by Cook and Campbell (1979) to describe the various ways in which uncontrolled or extraneous factors can present alternative explanations of research outcomes. These alternative explanations can rival or conceal the presumed true effect—the effect of the independent variable on the dependent variable. Consequently, the most scientifically credible research designs should rule out these alternative explanations or threats to our ability to make inferences. Campbell and Stanley outlined the major types of experimental designs and how each deals with the various threats to validity.

These threats to validity can be grouped in two broad categories. Eight possible threats to internal validity directly compete with our evaluation of the effects of the independent variables. The four possible threats to external validity deal with the generalizability of the results to settings other than that which is directly studied.

Threats to Internal Validity

Attrition refers to the fact that not all respondents who are present at the beginning of the experiment will be present for subsequent testing or measurement. Some respondents may move away, die, have scheduling conflicts, or simply choose not to appear for the study. If the attrition or loss of respondents is random or nonsystematic, it typically does not present a problem for interpreting the study's results. However, if differential attrition occurs—for example, certain kinds of respondents (e.g., low-income persons) are more likely to leave the study than others—it can complicate interpreting the effects on the dependent variable.

History refers to naturally occurring events that may affect the outcome of the study. For example, if your study was on the effectiveness of a series of television public-service announcements about family violence, and during the study a celebrity was arrested for assaulting his wife, this naturally occurring event could change the reactions of your television audience to the announcements.

Instrumentation deals with changes in the measurement instruments or operations. Changing observers or measuring instruments over the course of the experiment may produce unintended effects on the dependent variable.

Maturation refers to changes in the participants as a result of time passing. Getting older and growing tired or hungry are examples of maturation; one's behavior changes as one ages or becomes tired, with possible effects on the dependent variable of interest.

Selection has to do with how respondents are assigned to treatment groups for the experiment. Selection is a particularly important problem if respondents are not assigned randomly. Imagine that a researcher is trying to evaluate the effectiveness of an anger-management training program for spouse abusers. Individuals are invited to participate in the program, but they cannot be required to do so. The spouse abusers who decide to participate are probably different in important ways from those who do not, and these differences could affect the outcome of the study.

Statistical regression can be a problem when respondents are assigned to groups based on extreme scores on a scale. It is well-known that individuals who score at the extremes on an instrument tend to exhibit change in their scores toward the mean or average value over time. For example, high scorers on a measure of aggression tend to have lower scores when retested, even though the individuals' aggressive tendencies may not have undergone any real change.

Sometimes simply responding to a questionnaire or other measuring instrument can produce changes in the respondents. **Testing effects** occur when respondents change their responses as a consequence of encountering the measuring instrument. For example, if answering questions about abortion causes respondents to rethink their attitudes about the issue, they may change their responses to the interview.

Finally, two or more threats to internal validity may combine to form what is known as an **interaction** effect. One common interaction effect is between selection and history. If participant assignment to control and experimental groups is not done at random (but instead the selection is done on the basis of some specific criterion such as school enrollment or place of residence), the participants may experience different histories that may appear to be effects of the manipulation.

Threats to External Validity

The **reactive effect of testing** refers to the possibility that responding to a pretest might affect the respondent's reaction to the experimental manipulation, making it difficult to generalize the results of the experiment to non-pretested populations. In the anger-management training program mentioned earlier, the study might begin by giving the respondents a pretest consisting of a number of scenarios describing arguments between spouses and asking them to indicate what they would do in that scenario. The pretests would be scored in terms of how often the respondents indicated that they might resort to violence. Then, the respondents receive the anger-management training. The pretest questionnaire could sensitize the respondents to react differently to the training from the way they would if they hadn't encountered the pretest. Because spouse abusers outside the experiment would probably not receive the pretest before undergoing the training program, those results might be different from those in the experiment.

Interaction of selection and treatment occurs especially when respondents are not randomly assigned to treatment conditions. Imagine that a community wishes to evaluate the effectiveness of a marriage-preparation course. Volunteers are solicited from the population of engaged couples in the community. It's likely that those couples who volunteer to participate in such a program are different in important ways from couples who do not: They are probably more highly motivated, have more free time, and may have a stronger commitment to their partners than those who do not volunteer. These differences may interact with the effects of the marriage-preparation course to produce misleading results. In this case, the program might look much more effective than it really is.

The **reactive effects of experimental arrangements** refer to the fact that people who are aware that they are in an experiment may behave differently than they would normally. Also known as the *Hawthorne Effect* (Roethlisberger & Dickson, 1939), this phenomenon results when the observational process causes the respondents to change their behaviors.

Multiple-treatment interference occurs in experiments where there are multiple treatments provided to the same set of respondents. In such studies, the effects of one treatment may be contingent on respondents having received some other treatment.

Dealing With Threats to Validity

Two techniques are unique to experimental designs that can eliminate or at least reduce many threats to internal validity. Creation of a **control group** provides a basis of comparison to a group (typically known as the **experimental group** or treatment group) that receives the experimental treatment. Control group members are typically treated in exactly the same way as those in the experimental group except for receiving the experimental treatment. (In some studies the control group receives a placebo treatment designed to create the impression that they are receiving some type of experimental treatment.) At the end of the experiment, scores on the dependent variable for the participants in the control group are compared to the scores of those in the experimental group. All things being equal, differences between the responses of the control and experimental groups may be evidence of a genuine effect of the experimental treatment.

One problem with conducting experiments is ensuring that the participants' characteristics in the experimental and control groups are the same. In other words, at the start of the experiment, the control and experimental groups must be as nearly equivalent as possible. Otherwise, it may be difficult to conclude that any differences observed at the end of the experiment were really because of the effects of the experimental treatment (as opposed to some preexisting differences between the two groups). **Random assignment** is the primary technique used to achieve this equivalence. Assigning participants to the control and experimental groups randomly—especially when the groups are not excessively small—tends to create groups that are similar with respect to both measured and unmeasured characteristics. Without the use of control groups and random assignment, the results of experiments can be difficult to interpret. Campbell and Stanley (1963) distinguished between what they call **quasi-experimental designs**—which have some kind of control or comparison group but do not use random assignment to create the groups— and true **experimental designs,** which use randomization. Schutt (1999) presented a good introductory treatment of these experimental design issues.

Studying Families Through Survey Methods

Most of us have had some experience with survey methods. If you're like me, you probably get several mailings or phone calls a month asking questions about what products you buy or which candidates you support. The mailed questionnaire has become an unwelcome guest in our mailboxes. Maybe you have even had an interviewer come to your home or place of work to ask you questions directly. It's hard to miss the barrage of survey results on all manner of current events that appear in our magazines, newspapers, and the broadcast media.

Most survey research—regardless of whether the data are gathered by mail, over the phone, on the Internet, or in person—has three basic elements in common. First, survey research usually involves a relatively large number of respondents chosen to represent the population of interest. For most social research and public opinion polls, these samples are derived through probability sampling, most often some type of stratified random sample (sampling issues are discussed in Chapter 8). Second, the questions themselves are usually (but not always) closed-ended questions: The respondent is asked a question and given a limited number of possible responses from which to choose. Third, the responses are usually numerically coded and analyzed using computer software.

In comparing the major formats of survey research—mailed questionnaires, telephone interviews, and personal interviews—I want to focus consideration around four major concerns: **response rate** (what percentage of the sample will actually respond to our questions), potential for **interviewer bias** (where the interviewer's characteristics affect the respondents' responses to the survey instrument), opportunities for flexibility and quality control, and cost.

Mailed Questionnaires

We all receive questionnaires in the mail. Some are from legitimate researchers; some are from political organizations seeking to bolster their candidate's standing; most are from marketing-research organizations promoting a product or gathering information to aid them in their marketing strategies. Mailed questionnaires are by far the least expensive survey format because they don't incur telephone expenses or interviewer or travel costs.

Minton and Pasley (1996) compared parenting styles of nondivorced fathers to divorced, nonresidential fathers using mailed questionnaires to 270 fathers. Their results indicated that divorced fathers felt less competent and less satisfied in their parenting role than nondivorced fathers.

Although the presentation of the questionnaire is standardized (that is, no interviewer variations bias the respondent), certain populations are less likely to respond to mailed questionnaires. Those with poor reading skills, those who don't know the language of the questionnaire, and members of disadvantaged groups are less likely to respond to mailed questionnaires, thus creating significant problems of under- or overrepresentation of various groups.

The response rate to mailed questionnaires tends to be relatively low; even with repeated follow-ups, it is difficult to exceed a 75% response rate in surveys of the general public. Surveys of specialized populations—for example, members of a professional organization or graduates of a particular university—tend to have better rates of response. Adding to the nonresponses of those who fail to return the questionnaire at all are those who respond only to some items in the questionnaire, a behavior that is more common in mailed questionnaire research than in the other formats.

Mailed questionnaires may be the optimal choice (a) when the researcher must keep costs to a minimum and is willing to tolerate relatively low response rates and (b) when the topic of the questionnaire is relatively straightforward. One key drawback to mailed questionnaires is that the lack of interaction between the researcher and the respondent, which excludes the possibility of in-depth questioning and clarification of questions, makes it difficult to ask questions about complex behaviors and attitudes.

Telephone Interviews

Conducting survey research by telephone offers several benefits. First, the costs are relatively low; although generally more expensive than mailed questionnaires, telephone surveys are significantly cheaper than face-to-face interviews. Second, the ability of the researcher to directly oversee the interviewing staff and answer questions in real time allows a high degree of quality control over the process. Telephone surveys also tend to have relatively high response rates.

Although the use of random-digit dialing allows for contacting individuals with unlisted numbers, an obvious major disadvantage of telephone surveys is that the potential respondent must have a telephone to be interviewed. We tend to think of telephone ownership as a sort of universal constant, but less than 94% of American households have telephones. About one in four low-income households does not have telephone service, creating the potential for serious bias in the kinds of populations that can be meaningfully studied.

Aided by the development of computer-assisted interviewing, the technology for doing large-scale survey research in a cost-effective fashion has emerged quickly over the last 20 years. The integration of computers and telephone systems has enabled researchers to conduct nationwide surveys quickly and efficiently. If the potential bias created by variations in telephone ownership across populations is not a consideration, telephone interviews may be the method of choice. Buchanan, Maccoby, and Dornbusch (1991) used telephone interviews with 522 adolescents approximately 4.5 years after their parents divorced to study whether the children felt *caught* between their parents. Not surprisingly, they found that children were most likely to feel caught when their parents were in high conflict and least likely to feel caught when their parents cooperated.

Personal Interviews

Personal or face-to-face interviews are by far the most expensive mode of survey research. Costs of training interviewers and getting them to the respondents' homes or workplaces, especially in national samples, can be extremely high. Balanced against this high cost, however, are a number of distinct advantages. First, response rates tend to be relatively high. Second, the presence of the interviewer allows for the use of open-ended questions. Third, the interviewer can easily apply skip patterns (when certain questions are skipped contingent on the response to prior questions). Fourth, the interviewer can clarify questions that the respondent does not understand and probe if the response is unclear or superficial. Finally, interviews that are too long to be practical using mailed questionnaires or telephone interviews can often be accomplished using personal interviews.

Two other issues complicate the use of personal interviews. First, interviewers may introduce bias into the interview process (see the discussion about nonreactive measures that follows for some examples). Also, many types of respondents may be difficult to locate; young minority males, for example, are especially difficult to find at home. If sufficient funds are available, however, personal interviews are clearly the survey method of choice. Secret and Peck-Heath (2004) conducted personal interviews with 97 mothers, drawn from a random sample of public assistance recipients, to study the relationship between maternal employment and child well-being. In general, children whose mothers were employed had better health than children whose mothers had been unemployed for at least two years. Interestingly, children had better school performance if their mothers had either long-term employment or long-term unemployment, suggesting that the stability of maternal employment (rather than work status) was the key factor.

Surveys Over the Internet

According to Dillman (2000), "The two most significant advances in survey methodology during the 20th century were the introduction of random sampling in the 1940s and interviewing by telephone in the 1970s" (p. 352). The use of the Internet to collect survey data—through e-mailed questionnaires or interactive sites on the World Wide Web—promises to be equally important, perhaps even revolutionary.

Although e-mailed surveys are relatively limited in their ability to present complex survey questions and branching options—they are really mailed questionnaires delivered electronically rather than on paper through the mail—interactive Web-based surveys have a number of attractive features. First, they are inexpensive; other than the instrument development and data processing, for which costs are incurred in any type of survey, the only costs involved are those for the hosting of the Web site itself. Second, the questions can offer sophisticated interaction between the respondent and the questionnaire. Complex skips and branches in the flow of questions can be easily programmed into the questionnaire but remain invisible to the respondent. Drop-down boxes with large numbers of choices simplify responses; pop-up menus can offer clarification. Graphics and audio-video information can easily be incorporated into the questionnaire.

For all their advantages, Web-based surveys have notable disadvantages, too. Some possible respondents may not have the computer hardware and software required to handle cutting-edge Web sites. Some Web sites may appear differently on different kinds of browser software. By far the most serious problem, however, is presented by inequalities in access to the World Wide Web. Recent research (National Telecommunications and Information Administration, 1999) suggested that large differences in Web use and access may exist by social class, race, and gender. In 1999, only about one quarter of U.S. households had online access. Consequently, current Web-based surveys are likely to draw responses disproportionately from white, male, upper-middle-class respondents; but this situation is likely to change as online access becomes more widely available.

A recent example of a Web-based survey is provided by Lannutti's (2005) study of the meanings of same-sex marriage. In this study, 288 respondents were asked open-ended questions about how they thought legal recognition of same-sex marriage might affect the lesbian, gay, bisexual, and transgendered community.

Other Modes of Survey Research

Some survey research involves leaving with respondents the questionnaires that will be picked up later or mailed back to the researcher. Other techniques involve having groups of respondents (e.g., in a classroom or workplace) complete questionnaires with researcher supervision. Both techniques allow some face-to-face contact with the respondent to clarify questionnaire items.

There is a lot of bad survey research out there. So-called push polls, usually conducted by political polling organizations, are designed not so much to gather public opinion but to shape it. The questionnaire items are written to increase positive responses about the chosen candidate or issue; the survey results are then used to prop up the candidate or issue in the press. Perhaps the worst example of such a questionnaire came across my desk recently. My wife had her car serviced by a local dealer; and along with her itemized statement, she received a sample of a service survey that customers might get in the mail from the car's manufacturer asking questions about the service quality. On the sample questionnaire, all the *completely satisfied* or otherwise highly positive responses were checked (in red ink, no less!). One has to wonder whether such a procedure produces valid information about customer satisfaction or whether the real purpose is to merely produce glowing responses about the dealership's service department.

The issue of questionnaire design has been the subject of many books and articles. Schutt (1999) and Dillman (2000) presented detailed discussions of the major concerns in constructing questionnaires and other types of survey instruments.

Studying Families Through Observation

One popular method of studying families and children is through observation. Particularly in the study of very young children, observation can be a useful tool. Observational techniques are often used during the early stages of research as an exploratory tool. Let's say that you wanted to understand how free-forming playgroups work among preschoolers. This is an ideal problem for observational techniques, because your potential respondents probably cannot communicate the kinds of information you'd like to obtain through interviews (some may not even talk yet) or questionnaires.

As an example of an observational study, Amato (1989) observed children younger than 5 years of age and their primary caretaker in three types of naturalistic settings: recreational settings, commercial settings, and restaurants. Amato found that male caretaking was more likely when the child was male, in recreational settings, and with older children.

Five Criteria

We all observe behavior; we're all people watchers. And, as I pointed out in the first chapter, we are all more or less motivated to answer the why question: Why do people behave the way they do? However, if we all observe human behavior, what makes observation a scientific data collection technique?

Observation becomes a scientific tool when five criteria are met:

1. *The observation must serve a specific research purpose.* Simply sitting and observing—even if you take careful notes—isn't scientific research. The observation must be designed to accomplish a particular goal. In the study of free-forming playgroups described earlier, the researcher probably begins with only a rudimentary knowledge of the behavior of preschoolers and their playgroups. Observing preschoolers at play over time might sensitize the researcher to the key variables that are implicated in the process.

2. *The observation must be planned systematically.* To be a useful scientific tool, the observation must be planned systematically. At what times and on what days will you observe? It probably makes a difference if you observe preschoolers early in the morning (when they're still sleepy or perhaps suffering from separation anxiety after their parents have dropped them off at a day

care center) or late in the afternoon (when they're tired) or on Mondays (when they're trying to reacclimate to their day care environment after a weekend at home). Because the nature of the observational technique tends to limit the amount of observation to take place, the researcher must plan the timing of the observations carefully.

The observational researcher also has to have some idea of what to look for. Although some writers suggest that observers should enter the situation de novo (that is, without preconceptions or expectations), it's impossible to begin the observation without some expectations. It's important to ensure that these preconceptions don't structure your observations to the point that you miss the critical events and processes taking place.

3. *The observation is recorded systematically.* It is a truism that if we are to understand anything, we must give up hope of understanding everything. Observational research is no exception to this rule. It is impossible to record every aspect of an event: every spoken word, every gesture, every raised eyebrow. The observational researcher must make conscious decisions about which aspects of the event to record and how to record them. Bakeman and Gottman (1997) argued that the first step in observational research is to develop a coding scheme, which serves as "the lens through which [the researcher] has chosen to view the world" (p. 15). The three primary technologies for these recordings are written notes, audio or video recordings, or memory.

Some field researchers take what are known as *field jottings*: "phrases, quotes, keywords, and the likely to put down during the observation" (Lofland & Lofland, 1984). Most field researchers also write up *field notes* as soon as possible following each observation period.

4. *The observation is related to general propositions rather than specific examples.* The sociological literature is filled with case studies. However interesting these case studies might be, however, they are not of great scientific value unless they are related to general propositions derived from theories or specific hypotheses about general processes. This is perhaps the most important distinction between sociological research and journalism. To the journalist, the subject of the case study is interesting in and of itself. For the sociologist, although the case study may be interesting, it is primarily a means to an end: evidence to be used to test the validity of a general proposition, theory, or hypothesis.

5. *The observation is subjected to checks on reliability and validity.* Sometimes it is said that because the researcher is part of the setting, issues such as reliability and validity are not important in observational research. Or

you might hear the argument that observational research is somehow more valid than other research strategies. Despite these claims, issues of reliability and validity are just as important in observational research as they are in other research strategies. The issue of consistency among different observers is of particular importance.

Imagine, for example, an observational study of aggressive behavior among 3-year-olds. Part of the project involves coding nonverbal aggressive behaviors on the part of the children. The observer may be asked to make subjective decisions about which nonverbal behaviors should be coded as aggressive and which ones should not. If this measurement is truly reliable (in the sense of consistency), different observers should agree which nonverbal behaviors should be coded as aggressive and which ones should not.

Studying Families Through Nonreactive Techniques

Experiments, surveys, and observational techniques all intrude on the respondent's world. Consequently, they may affect the responses that, in turn, may impair the validity of our findings. A **nonreactive technique** attempts to remove the researcher from the setting or behavior being studied. Nonreactive techniques (sometimes called *unobtrusive* techniques) are designed to avoid intruding on the respondent's world. The errors that reactive or obtrusive research designs create can be examined in terms of whether they are introduced by the respondent or by the researcher.

Four Kinds of Errors Introduced by the Respondent

1. *The Guinea Pig Effect.* When people know that they are participating in a research project, they may alter their behavior. When we know people are watching us, our behavior may be different from when we think we are alone and unobserved.

2. *Role Selection.* People who are participating in research projects sometimes role-play or act the way they think the researcher wants them to act. Knowing that they were selected because they were members of a dysfunctional family, participants in a study on dysfunctional families might respond in unusual and unpredictable ways to an interviewer's questions. If, instead, potential respondents had simply been told that they would be participating in a general study about families, they might have given more valid responses.

3. *Measurement as Change Agent.* Sometimes, the research instrument itself can create change in the people it is studying. Perhaps the respondent might

be asked questions about the appropriateness of child day care for children younger than 3 years old. A particular respondent might not have thought about this problem before, but being confronted with these questions might lead the respondent to form opinions on the spot—opinions the respondent, if not asked the questions, might not have formulated.

4. *Response Sets.* Respondents in a research study don't always respond honestly to the interviewer's questions. Sometimes, respondents tend to agree with statements, no matter how the statements are worded; this is known as the **acquiescence response set.** This response set is sometimes avoided with pairs of items constructed so that a respondent's agreement with both items represents an apparent contradiction that is apparent to the researcher.

Some respondents feel the need to make a good impression to present a favorable image to others. Such respondents may give what they believe to be the correct or socially acceptable responses to the questions. This type of response set is known as **social desirability.** It is well-known, for example, that respondents overreport such socially acceptable behaviors as voting and underreport unacceptable behaviors such as child abuse. Studies of family life are particularly susceptible to problems with social desirability because of strong social norms about what constitutes a good family or good parenting. Many respondents may be unwilling to admit to behaviors that contradict these social norms.

Ordinal biases (also called positional biases) represent a third type of response set. Here, the order in which the questions are asked may affect the responses obtained.

Three Kinds of Errors Introduced by the Researcher

1. *Interviewer Effects.* Subtle and not-so-subtle aspects of the interviewer's demeanor and appearance can affect responses to our research. Imagine how the race of the interviewer might affect responses to questions about race relations or how the results of interviews about police brutality conducted by police officers might be influenced. Even such factors as style of dress and variations in speaking styles (accents, grammar) might affect responses to an interview. In studies of families, the race and gender are potential sources of bias. Ethnic respondents may not be forthcoming about their family practices with outsiders, and some white respondents might be less than candid with interviewers of other races. Both male and female respondents might be unwilling to share the details of their intimate relationships with opposite-sex interviewers.

2. *Changes in the Instrument.* It's difficult to keep social science instruments constant over time. Interviewers change inflections; questions may have to be reworded in light of current events; alternate questionnaire versions may be necessary to avoid the biases created by response sets. When such changes occur, it is always problematic to discern whether the effects on the dependent variable are caused by the independent variable under study or are artifacts created by changes in the instrument.

3. *Population Restrictions.* It's not always obvious how much the data collection technique can affect the composition of the sample under study. We tend to think of the telephone as present in every U.S. household, but one in four central city households with incomes less than $5,000 doesn't have a telephone (National Telecommunications and Information Administration, 1999). Clearly, using telephone interviews biases the sample away from low-income households.

Mailed questionnaires are also problematic for some populations, because they require the respondent to be able to read and have good enough English-language skills to understand and respond to the questions (not to mention having a mailing address). If the researcher doesn't provide interviewers fluent in languages other than English or alternative versions of the questionnaire, a sizable percentage of U.S. households will be eliminated from the sample; the 1990 Census indicates that as many as 3.1% of all adults in the United States do not speak English well enough for a survey interview.

Types of Nonreactive Research

Physical Traces

Human beings often leave behind evidence of their behaviors, often unaware that they've done so. When this evidence takes the form of selective wear or degradation of artifacts, it is known as **erosion.** When the evidence takes the form of the selective deposit of materials, it is known as **accretion.**

Erosion measures refer to selective wear that yields data that may be used to test theories or hypotheses about behavior. Some examples of erosion measures include assessing the popularity of museum exhibits by measuring the amount of wear on the flooring, use of library materials by assessing deterioration of bindings, and use of particular sites on the Internet by assessing the degradation of response time for the Web site's server.

Accretion measures deal with a selective deposit of materials. Whenever anthropologists study pottery shards, they are studying the selective deposit of materials unknowingly left behind by the people who made them. Other examples of accretion measures include estimating radio audiences by noting the stations to which car radios are tuned when they come in for service, studying the social class of the clientele of entertainment establishments by noting the book value of cars parked outside, and measuring alcohol consumption in various portions of the city by counting the number of empty liquor bottles found in trash bins.

The Running Record

All large organizations keep records, many of which—government records in particular—are open to the public by law. Other kinds of records—in the mass media, in particular—are public by their very nature.

Actuarial records are kept by many government agencies. More than half a century ago, Winston (1932) studied the preference for male offspring in upper-class families. His research design could have involved interviewing pregnant women, interviewing prospective fathers in hospital waiting rooms, or perhaps paying obstetricians to ask expectant couples about their gender preference. Instead, he chose a nonreactive design that involved analyzing birth records to determine whether the last-born children in such families were males more often than is likely to occur by chance, thus suggesting a preference for male children.

Political and judicial records provide much data for research in the social sciences. Criminal-court records have long been used to study racial bias in sentencing procedures. Divorce-court records might be used to study the effects of various factors on child custody decisions. Carmichael (1985) used court records from New Zealand to show that women have been more likely to be awarded formal custody in recent years.

The mass media are often used to study trends in the public's perception of marriage and family issues. Middleton (1960) compared actual family sizes (based on government statistics) to ideal family sizes (based on fictional stories about families that appeared in popular magazines) and found that shifts in ideal family sizes tended to parallel shifts in actual family sizes. Atkinson and Blackwelder (1993) studied images of fathers in popular magazines using a similar strategy.

Advantages of the Running Record

Using the running record offers three major advantages. First, such data exists in large quantities. Certain vital statistics in the United States, for example, have been collected for more than 200 years. Much of this data are collected annually, simplifying analyses of trends over time. The second major advantage of using the running record is cost. Most governmental and mass media records are available at no cost or simply for the cost of duplicating the material. And, third, these are nonreactive techniques: Using them for research purposes is relatively nonintrusive.

Using the running record also has some disadvantages. One is the problem of **selective deposit**. Some data may never get into the public record; the court, for example, may seal birth records of adoptees. Second, **selective survival** is a problem. Inevitably, some records get lost or destroyed. Others may be deliberately removed. As a favor to a friend, for example, a police officer might remove information about an act of domestic violence from the criminal record.

The Episodic and Private Record

Records kept by individuals and private organizations are not usually part of the public record and are not generally kept continuously or over long periods of time. However, they still may represent a valuable source of research materials for the researcher who can gain access to them.

Sales records are often a good unobtrusive indicator of public opinion. Airline passenger anxiety, for example, might be measured by alcohol sales at airports or by air-travel insurance policy sales. Sales of burglar alarm systems might indicate public fear of crime. Sales of various over-the-counter contraceptive techniques could represent their relative popularity.

Industrial and institutional records may be used to investigate a wide range of research topics. Here, the primary problem is one of entrée. Most businesses are not eager to share their internal records with outsiders, and when they do they often limit the types or amount of access to internal documents.

Content analysis of personal written documents is among the most well-known nonreactive or unobtrusive methods. Thomas and Znaniecki's (1918) classic *The Polish Peasant in Europe and America* content-analyzed letters written home by Polish immigrants to study the acculturation process at the turn of the century. Janowitz (1958) studied the effects of Allied propaganda during World War II by studying letters and diaries written by Axis prisoners of war.

Secondary Analysis of Sample Surveys

Perusing journals that publish family research, you may notice that many researchers didn't collect their own data: They used data collected by other researchers or agencies, often for very different research purposes. Chapter 11 is devoted to a presentation of **secondary analysis** and discusses many of the most popular data sets used for such research.

Some Limitations of Quantitative Methods

It should be apparent that the methods described in this chapter—experiments, surveys, observation, nonreactive techniques, and secondary analysis of sample surveys—are all relatively structured. The quantitative researcher begins the research process by phrasing one or more research questions or hypotheses, which structure the nature of both the sample and the data collection instruments and techniques. The sample, instruments, and techniques can have the effect of limiting the types of knowledge that can be gathered or can even affect the outcome of the study. For example, if a written questionnaire is used, only those with some fluency (and reading ability) in the language can be studied. For a mailed questionnaire, only those with valid addresses can be surveyed. Telephone surveys may eliminate lower-income individuals and families from the study, because they are least likely to have telephone service in their homes. Another problem created by this structure is a limitation on what can be learned from respondents. In a mailed questionnaire, once the questionnaires have been sent to potential respondents, it's too late to add a new question or follow-up on an existing one.

A body of techniques referred to as **qualitative research** present an alternative to traditional quantitative methods. In contrast to the relatively structured approaches of surveys, experiments, and structured interviews, qualitative methods emphasize the unfolding nature of the research process. Chapter 7 presents an introduction to qualitative methods of studying families. Chapter 8 discusses the possibilities of what are known as **mixed-methods studies,** the combination of quantitative and qualitative methods in the same study to improve our understanding of some social phenomenon.

Study Questions

1. Find one example of each of the following quantitative research strategies in any of the major family-related journals: experiment, sample survey, observation, and nonreactive methods. Briefly describe the research technique in each article.

2. Using one of the studies you located in the first question, critique the research method using whatever criteria you feel are appropriate.

3. Choose a family-related topic of interest to you, and present brief (about one paragraph) descriptions of how you might study that topic using each of the following: (a) an experiment, (b) a sample survey, (c) an observational study, and (d) a nonreactive method.

For Further Reading

Amato, P. R. (1989). Who cares for children in public places—Naturalistic observation of male and female caretakers. *Journal of Marriage and the Family, 51,* 981–990.

Atkinson, M. P., & Blackwelder, S. P. (1993). Fathering in the 20th-century. *Journal of Marriage and the Family, 55,* 975–986.

Bakeman, R., & Gottman, J. M. (1997). *Observing interaction: An introduction to sequential analysis.* New York: Cambridge University Press.

Bridges, J. S., & Orza, A. M. (1993). Effects of maternal employment-childrearing pattern on college students' perceptions of a mother and her child. *Psychology of Women Quarterly, 17,* 103–117.

Buchanan, C. M., Maccoby, E. E., & Dornbusch, S. M. (1991). Caught between parents: Adolescents' experience in divorced homes. *Child Development, 62,* 1008–1029.

Campbell, D. T., & Stanley, J. C. (1963). *Experimental and quasi-experimental designs for research.* Chicago: Rand McNally.

Carmichael, G. A. (1985). Children and divorce in New Zealand. *Journal of Marriage and the Family, 47,* 221–231.

Cook, T. D., & Campbell, D. T. (1979). *Quasi-experimentation: Design & analysis issues for field settings.* Boston: Houghton Mifflin.

Dillman, D. A. (2000). *Mail and Internet surveys: The tailored design method.* New York: John Wiley & Sons.

Hannan, M. T., Tuma, N. B., & Groeneveld, L. P. (1978). Income and independence effects on marital dissolution: Results from the Seattle and Denver income-maintenance experiments. *American Journal of Sociology, 84,* 611–633.

Janowitz, M. (1958). Inferences about propaganda impact from textual and documentary analysis. In W. E. Daugherty & M. Janowitz (Eds.), *A psychological warfare casebook* (pp. 732–735). Baltimore: Johns Hopkins Press.

Lannutti, P. (2005). For better or worse: Exploring the meanings of same-sex marriages within the lesbian, gay, bisexual and transgendered community. *Journal of Personal and Social Relationships, 22,* 5–18.

Lofland, J., & Lofland, L. H. (1984). *Analyzing social settings: A guide to qualitative observation and analysis.* Belmont, CA: Wadsworth.

Middleton, R. (1960). Fertility values in American magazine fiction: 1916–1956. *Public Opinion Quarterly, 24,* 139–143.

Minton, C., & Pasley, K. (1996). Fathers' parenting role identity and father involvement: A comparison of nondivorced and divorced, nonresident fathers. *Journal of Family Issues, 17,* 26–45.

National Telecommunications and Information Administration. (1999). *Falling through the net: Defining the digital divide.* Washington, DC: Government Printing Office.

Roethlisberger, F. J., & Dickson, W. I. (1939). *Management and the worker: An account of a research program conducted by the Western Electric Co. Hawthorne Works, Chicago.* Cambridge, MA: Harvard University Press.

Schutt, R. K. (1999). *Investigating the social world: The process and practice of research.* Thousand Oaks, CA: Pine Forge.

Secret, M., & Peck-Heath, C. (2004). Maternal labor force participation and child well-being in public assistance families. *Journal of Family Issues, 25,* 520–541.

Thomas, W. I., & Znaniecki, F. (1918). *The Polish peasant in Europe and America.* Boston: Gorham Press.

Winston, S. (1932). Birth control and the sex-ratio at birth. *American Journal of Sociology, 38,* 225–231.

7

Studying Families:
Qualitative Methods

In Chapter 6, I pointed out that quantitative research strategies such as surveys and experiments tend to be highly structured. Traditional structured interviews or questionnaires often inadequately assess the underlying justifications or motives people have for their everyday behavior. For example, a typical survey question in studies of housework is to ask women whether they think that the division of household labor in their family is fair. From their responses, we can determine how many wives say that the division of household labor in their family is fair and how many say that it is unfair. However, from such survey responses, we get little insight into why a particular wife feels that the division of household labor in her family is fair or unfair. Is it because she feels she does too much housework or because her husband does too little? Is she comparing the amount of housework she does to the amount done by her husband or to other wives that she knows? What does she mean by fair? What activities does she consider housework?

These are the kinds of questions that **qualitative research** methods excel at answering, those perhaps only answerable through the kinds of in-depth observation and interviews discussed in this chapter. Qualitative strategies tend to be relatively unstructured, and many qualitative methodologies argue against researchers imposing their own structures on the data. Punch (1998) suggested that quantitative data may be defined as "empirical information in the form of numbers." Qualitative data, however, are "information about the world in the form of words" (p. 59).

Daly (1992) suggested that qualitative methods are especially valuable for family researchers because "the focus is not on identifying structural or demographic trends in families, but rather on the processes by which families create, sustain, and discuss their own family realities" (p. 4). In Chapter 1, I identified an important difference between social research in general and research on families: Families are groups or systems of individuals. This emphasis on holistic understanding makes qualitative methods especially well suited to studying families.

Qualitative Research
Compared to Quantitative Research

From even a casual reading of the literature on qualitative research methods, clearly the goals of qualitative methods are substantially different from those of the quantitative techniques discussed in Chapter 6. These goals are the result of radically different epistemological orientations about the relationship of theory and research. Epistemological orientations may be thought of as assumptions "about how to know the social and apprehend its meaning"

(Fonow & Cook, 1991, p. 4). The researcher's epistemological orientation affects the topics studied, the types of questions asked, and the methods employed to answer these questions.

Generally speaking, quantitative methods are employed in the sequence described in Chapter 1: exploration, description, prediction, explanation, intervention, and evaluation. Knowledge concerning the phenomenon of interest develops gradually but systematically, and hypotheses are derived from extant theory or empirical generalizations. Theory and hypotheses, then, precede the research process. This perspective is often referred to as *postpositivism* (Popper, 1964, 1992). Theory determines the choice of concepts to be studied and the procedures employed to measure those concepts.

Many qualitative researchers pursue a much different course, however, following what might be called a *constructionist* or *phenomenological* approach. Daly (1992) suggested that qualitative methods in family studies follow Weber's (1947) *verstehen* tradition and that "qualitative methods are suited to understanding the meanings, interpretations, and subjective experiences of family members (pp. 1–2). Gilgun (1992) defined qualitative family research as having "a focus on experiences within families as well as between families and outside systems" (p. 24).

The *grounded theory* school of thought (Glaser & Strauss, 1967; Straus & Corbin, 1990) argues that theory can *emerge* from the data. Although a comprehensive comparison of grounded theory to positivist approaches is beyond the scope of this text, Punch (1998) pointed out that although traditional quantitative methods have usually emphasized a theory-verification model— that is, using research to test theories—grounded theory advocates a theory-generation model. In the theory-generation model, research findings precede theory, and researchers typically don't approach their research with specific hypotheses in mind. The grounded-theory approach, therefore, is most advantageous when there is no well-developed theory about the phenomenon of interest. For more discussion of the application of grounded theory to research on families, see Gilgun (1992). In addition, Cauhapé (1983) presented an interesting example of grounded theory applied to the study of men and women after divorce.

Not all quantitative research, however, is positivistic, and not all qualitative research follows the constructivist or phenomenological approaches.

Types of Qualitative Strategies

Despite many different styles of qualitative methods, Punch (1998, pp. 148–149) argued that a hallmark of qualitative research is that it is naturalistic—it tends to study people and groups in their natural settings. Although some forms of quantitative research are clearly naturalistic—observational techniques and some of the nonreactive techniques that gather data in natural settings—most (such as surveys and experiments) are not. Miles and Huberman (1994, pp. 6–7) suggested eight recurring elements in qualitative research:

1. Qualitative research is conducted through intense and prolonged contact with the context under study.

2. The goal of the researcher is to gain a holistic overview of the context under study.

3. The researcher attempts to understand the context from the standpoint of the participants themselves rather than from the researcher's own perspective.

4. Although the research may, over time, isolate certain themes that may be reviewed with the participants themselves, the field notes and observations should be maintained in their original forms throughout the study.

5. A primary goal of qualitative research is to understand the ways that people come to understand, account for, take action, and otherwise manage their day-to-day activities.

6. Whereas many interpretations of the field notes are possible, some are more compelling than others for theoretical reasons or for reasons of internal consistency.

7. Relatively little standardized instrumentation is used.

8. Most analysis is done with words (as opposed to numbers).

Despite many different ways to organize the various types of naturalistic qualitative-research strategies, thinking in terms of four broad groupings that typically use different approaches is useful: case studies, ethnographies, time diary methods, and focus groups.

Case Studies

A case study is typically an intensive, in-depth study of a few cases—often a single case—where the goal is "to develop as full an understanding of that case as possible" (Punch, 1998, p. 150). Miles and Huberman (1994) defined a case as "a phenomenon of some sort occurring in a bounded context" (p. 25). In family research, the case under study is typically a single family or group of families who share some common trait (for example, families headed by Latinos, single-parent families, or families with employed mothers), but it can also be individuals, dyads (couples), or even communities or organizations.

In an example of a case study where families were the unit of analysis, Risman and Johnson-Sumerford (1998) studied the families of 15 married couples who divided housework and child care equitably and regardless of gender "to determine how they arrived at this arrangement and what consequences such a distribution of household labor has on their relationship" (p. 23). For each family, a team, consisting of an interviewer for each parent and one for each child older than age 4 years, interviewed the family members independently in their own home. The interviews lasted from one to more than three hours and were tape recorded and transcribed verbatim. Each interviewer also contributed field notes and an analytic summary to the interview. One member of the team also observed the family in their home from the time the parents arrived home from work until the children were asleep.

An example of a case study where the unit of analysis is the organization is Hochschild's (1997) examination of family-friendly policies at Amerco, a Fortune 500 corporation located in the Midwest. She interviewed 130 employees at all levels within the corporation and talked with psychologists, child care workers, and spouses of employees. She also did day-long observations of six families of Amerco employees.

The Risman and Johnson-Sumerford study is a **multiple-case study**; Hochschild's is a **single-case study**. With these examples in mind, and drawing on the discussions of Punch (1998) and Yin (1994), we can suggest two basic characteristics of case studies in general. First, the focus of a case study is an example of something: a particular type of individual, family, or organization. The specific case is usually selected because it is presumed to typify similar cases; examination of that particular case can help illuminate the nature of similar cases.

Second, the researcher is likely to use multiple sources of data and methods of data collection. Risman and Johnson-Sumerford's study, for example, used both personal interviews with the family members and unstructured observations of the family going about their everyday lives. Hochschild, in her effort to understand how Amerco employees attempted to resolve conflicts between work and family, used observations in the workplace, at home, and at a child care center; interviews with employees and their spouses; and corporate documents.

Drawing on Punch (1998), eight issues are important to consider when evaluating a case study:

1. What, exactly, is the case under study?

2. What are its boundaries?

3. What was the main purpose of the study?

4. What were the research questions in the study?

5. Did the study use single or multiple cases?

6. How were the data collected and from whom?

7. How were the data analyzed?

8. What were the findings or conclusions of the study?

Ethnographies

Probably the best-known text on ethnography is Hammersley and Atkinson's *Ethnography: Principles in Practice* (1995), which argued that the primary goal of ethnography is the description of cultures. In ethnographic research, observers are encouraged to make their preconceptions about the culture being studied explicit so "the culture is turned into an object available for study" (Hammersley & Atkinson, 1995, p. 10). Ethnographic research attempts to understand a culture or way of life from the point of view of its participants. In most ethnographic studies, the observer participates, over an extended period of time, in the lives of the people being studied. Thus, participant observation is a primary method of ethnographic research. The observer attempts to understand the events and meanings attributed to those events by the people being studied.

Although many of the best-known ethnographies are studies of cultures other than Western industrialized societies—for example, Margaret Mead's (1935) studies of New Guinea tribes—social and behavioral scientists also employ ethnographic methods to study groups close to home. Because ethnographic methods encourage the observer to deal explicitly with any preconceptions about the culture being studied, it is especially useful for the study of marginalized groups (for example, disadvantaged minorities, the homeless, abused wives) in our own society. A good example of ethnographic research in the family area is Carol Stack's (1974) study of kinship ties among African Americans.

Drawing again from Punch (1998, pp. 160–161), a number of distinguishing characteristics of ethnographic research can be identified.

- First, and perhaps most important, the group or phenomenon is studied in its natural setting. The observer must directly experience the physical and social world of those being studied.
- Second, the observer must be sensitive to the meanings that events have for those being studied. A primary goal of the research is to uncover these meanings. To do this, the observer has to take the perspective (standpoint) of those being studied.

- Third, the exact focus of the ethnography will often not be evident before beginning the study; consequently, structuring the data and developing instruments will often be done as the research proceeds, rather than before beginning the project.
- Although fieldwork and, especially, participant observation are central to most ethnographic research, other techniques (for example, structured interviews, questionnaires, content analyses) may be used as necessary and appropriate.
- Finally, ethnographic research is a long process. This is partially because it can take a long time for the observer to gain access to, and acceptance by, the group being studied and because "the ethnographic record needs to be comprehensive and detailed" (Punch, 1998, p. 161).

Time Diary Methods

Time-use diaries are often used when researchers want to collect information about how people spend their time, especially with regard to paid employment hours, leisure time, household work, and child care. The diaries can be completed during a personal or telephone interview or through a self-administered form mailed to or left with the respondent.

Bryant and Zick (1996, pp. 369–371) presented an interesting summary of time-use **diary studies** going back to the 1920s, when the U.S. Department of Agriculture did a series of studies asking women to keep time-use diaries for a week (Kneeland, 1929). The use of such methods has continued to the present day, for example in Robinson and Godbey's (1999) work on leisure time and Jacobs and Gerson's (2004) research on family time pressures.

There are actually a number of techniques used to gather estimates of time use. Beeper studies equip a respondent with a pager or *beeper* programmed to beep at random. The respondents are instructed to record what they were doing (and in some cases, what they were thinking) when the beeper goes off. Other researchers have used observational techniques to record time use in families (Coltrane, 1996; Levine et al., 2001).

In this literature, there is some debate as to the relative validity of different types of methods of measuring time use. Jacobs and Gerson (2004, pp. 15–18) presented a discussion of these issues, noting that some researchers (Robinson & Godbey, 1999) feel that time diaries provide more valid information because the diary entries are more detailed than the results of the other techniques. Others (Schor, 1991) contended that estimates based on time diaries are biased because the busiest people may be less likely to complete them. It may be that combinations of time-use data collection methods are necessary to obtain a complete picture of how people spend their time.

Focus Groups

Focus groups are small groups (usually 7–10 members) of individuals brought together to discuss a specific topic of interest to the researcher. A moderator leads and directs the discussion, but the process is essentially unstructured. Focus groups are used extensively in a number of areas for at least three purposes. Probably the best-known use of focus groups is in marketing research, which uses focus groups to gauge consumers' reactions to new products or advertising. Political consultants use focus groups to assess voter reactions to positions on issues and the relative attractiveness of candidates.

Social researchers use focus groups in either of two ways. First, the use of groups can aid development of instrumentation for more structured research techniques (e.g., telephone surveys or personal interviews). Second, the focus group's interactions may be used as qualitative data in their own right in the study of a particular topic (Morgan, 1997).

Krueger (1994) identified several key advantages offered by focus groups:

- A format for studying a topic in depth in a naturally occurring environment
- Flexibility
- High face validity
- Quick turnaround time from initiation to analysis of data
- Low cost

Yet, Krueger also pointed out some disadvantages of this technique:

- The researcher has less control over the kinds of information gathered than in more structured techniques such as personal interviews or questionnaires.
- Exactly how the qualitative data generated by the focus group should be analyzed is not always clear.
- The group moderator must be skillful at encouraging the group's conversation without forcing participants into specific directions or conclusions.
- Convening groups to discuss threatening or somewhat controversial topics may be difficult.
- Creating an environment that encourages open participation by all group members may be difficult.

Evaluating Qualitative Research

Although the structure imposed by quantitative methods can sometimes limit the researcher's ability to fully understand families, that same structure also provides security in the sense of well-established standards regarding the quality or soundness of research. A consensus among quantitative researchers is that we must be attentive to a number of key indicators of *good* research. Are the measures valid and reliable? Are the sampling procedures appropriate? Does the research design reduce the impact of extraneous factors and consider possible alternative interpretations? The design of the research and its instrumentation are determined by the theory. The theory suggests the appropriate unit of analysis and how the various concepts are measured.

In contrast to the relative consensus among quantitative research methods, qualitative methods in family research are characterized by a greater diversity in techniques and perspectives. Furthermore, what constitutes good qualitative research is open to a fair amount of controversy. Miles and Huberman (1994) wrote that qualitative methodologists "have this unappealing double bind whereby qualitative studies can't be verified because researchers don't report on their methodology, and they don't report on their methodology because there are no established canons or conventions for doing so" (p. 244). Gilgun (1992) suggested, "The downside of moving toward diversity of research methods, methodologies, and theories is insecurity. Qualitative researchers are prone to asking: Am I doing it right?" (p. 27). This is a problem that I (and I suspect many quantitative researchers) have when reading qualitative research studies: I'm never certain what, exactly, constitutes *good* qualitative research.

Gilgun (1992) argued that "a guideline for the conduct of qualitative research . . . is whether we are successful in communicating our processes and findings" (p. 27). Does the research faithfully communicate what the informants are saying? Is the research method getting in the way of what the informants are saying? These, of course, are exceedingly different questions from the ones that quantitative researchers would ask about their research.

In Chapter 8, I explore a possible reconciliation between the divergent philosophies and approaches of quantitative and qualitative strategies: mixed methods.

Study Questions

1. Find examples of each of the following qualitative research strategies in any of the major family-related journals: single-case study, multiple-case study, ethnography, time diary, and focus group. Briefly describe the research technique in each article.

2. Choose any one of the studies you located in the previous question, and critique the research method using whatever criteria you feel are appropriate.

3. Choose a family-related topic of interest to you, and present brief (about one paragraph) descriptions of how you might study that topic using (a) a case study, (b) an ethnography, (c) a diary study, and (d) a focus group.

For Further Reading

Bryant, W. K., & Zick, C. D. (1996). An examination of parent-child shared time. *Journal of Marriage and the Family, 58,* 227–237.

Cauhapé, E. (1983). *Fresh starts: Men and women after divorce.* New York: Basic Books.

Coltrane, S. (1996). *Family man: Fatherhood, housework, and gender equity.* New York: Oxford University Press.

Daly, K. (1992). The fit between qualitative research and characteristics of families. In J. F. Gilgun, K. Daly, & G. Handel (Eds.), *Qualitative methods in family research* (pp. 3–11). Beverly Hills, CA: Sage.

Fonow, M. M., & Cook, J. A. (1991). Back to the future: A look at the second wave of feminist epistemology and methodology. In M. M. Fonow & J. A. Cook (Eds.), *Beyond methodology: Feminist scholarship as lived experience* (pp. 1–15). Bloomington: Indiana University Press.

Gilgun, J. F. (1992). Definitions, methodologies, and methods in qualitative family research. In J. F. Gilgun, K. Daly, & G. Handel (Eds.), *Qualitative methods in family research* (pp. 22–40). Beverly Hills, CA: Sage.

Glaser, B. G., & Strauss, A. L. (1967). *The discovery of grounded theory: Strategies for qualitative research.* Chicago: Aldine.

Hammersley, M., & Atkinson, P. (1995). *Ethnography: Principles in practice* (2nd ed.). London, New York: Routledge.

Hochschild, A. R. (1997). *The time bind: When work becomes home and home becomes work.* New York: Metropolitan.

Jacobs, J. A., & Gerson, K. (2004). *The time divide: Work, family, and gender inequality.* Cambridge, MA: Harvard University Press.

Kneeland, H. (1929). Women's economic contributions in the home. *Annals of the American Academy, 143,* 33–40.

Krueger, R. A. (1994). *Focus groups: A practical guide for applied research* (2nd ed.). Thousand Oaks, CA: Sage.

Levine, J. A., Weisell, R., Chevassus, S., Martinez, C. D., Burlingame, B., & Coward, W. A. (2001). The work burden of women. *Science, 294,* 812.

Mead, M. (1935). *Sex and temperament in three primitive societies.* New York: W. Morrow.

Miles, M. B., & Huberman, A. M. (1994). *Qualitative data analysis: An expanded sourcebook* (2nd ed.). Thousand Oaks, CA: Sage.

Morgan, D. L. (1997). *Focus groups as qualitative research* (2nd ed.). Thousand Oaks, CA: Sage.

Popper, K. R. (1964). *The poverty of historicism.* New York: Harper & Row.

Popper, K. R. (1992). *The logic of scientific discovery.* London, New York: Routledge.

Punch, K. E. (1998). *Introduction to social research: Quantitative and qualitative approaches.* London: Sage.

Risman, B. J., & Johnson-Sumerford, D. (1998). Doing it fairly: A study of postgender marriages. *Journal of Marriage and the Family, 60,* 23–40.

Robinson, J. P., & Godbey, G. (1999). *Time for life: The surprising ways Americans use their time* (2nd ed.). University Park: Pennsylvania State University Press.

Schor, J. (1991). *The overworked American: The unexpected decline of leisure.* New York: Basic Books.

Stack, C. B. (1974). *All our kin: Strategies for survival in a black community.* New York: Harper & Row.

Straus, M. A., & Corbin, J. M. (1990). *Basics of qualitative research.* Newbury Park, CA: Sage.

Weber, M. (1947). *The theory of social and economic organization* (M. Henderson, & T. Parsons, Trans.). New York: Free Press.

Yin, R. K. (1994). *Case study research: Design and methods* (2nd ed.). Thousand Oaks, CA: Sage.

8

Studying Families: Mixed Methods

C hapter 6 (on quantitative methods) and Chapter 7 (on qualitative methods) might give you the impression that these are two totally different and mutually exclusive approaches to studying marriages and families. Indeed, some texts imply conflict between *quants* and *quals*; and to be honest, there is some animosity held by some members of each side.

Since the 1980s, **mixed methods** has emerged as an approach that combines elements of traditional quantitative techniques along with the qualitative. Compared to traditional quantitative approaches (which have their basis in postpositivism) and qualitative approaches (usually identified with constructivism or phenomenology), the mixed-method approach has its epistemological or philosophical roots in pragmatism (see Cherryhomes, 1992). Creswell (2003) suggested that for pragmatists, "There is a concern with applications— 'what works'—and solutions to problems. Instead of methods being important, the problem is most important; and researchers use all approaches to understand the problem" (p. 11). Not surprisingly, researchers adopting the pragmatist position are likely to choose from a wide range of research strategies, from the highly quantitative to the most qualitative.

Tashakkori and Teddlie (1998) suggested a threefold taxonomy of research studies. *Monomethod* studies use either quantitative or qualitative techniques (but not both) exclusively throughout the research process. Such studies may use multiple data sources, but only one methodological strategy is employed in a given study. Although Tashakkori and Teddlie suggest that social researchers have moved beyond monomethod approaches, a quick scan of any major family-related journal will show that most current research still uses either qualitative or quantitative approaches—but not both in the same study.

Mixed-Method Approaches to Family Research

Mixed-method studies combine qualitative and quantitative approaches in a single study. Such studies might be sequential, beginning with quantitative techniques (e.g., statistical analysis of census data), and proceed to qualitative methods (e.g., case studies or ethnographies) to further explore the meanings of the phenomena identified in the quantitative phase. Alternatively, the research might begin with qualitative work (such as personal interviews with a small number of informants) and then use large-scale quantitative methods (such as mailed questionnaires) to test hypotheses developed in the qualitative phase. Or the study might combine both qualitative and quantitative techniques simultaneously but at different levels of aggregation. For example, a researcher might do quantitative, statistical analyses of school-level, achievement test–score data while at the same time doing observational studies of student classroom performance.

Pearce's (2002) study of the effects of religion on fertility preferences provides an excellent example of the sequential mixed-method approach. She began with data from a probability sample of more than 5,000 residents of the Chitwan Valley in south-central Nepal. After developing a multiple regression model predicting family size preferences, she focused her attention on the respondents who expressed a desire for substantially larger families than that predicted by her model. She drew a random sample of 28 respondents from this group and conducted 90-minute interviews with each. This is the point where "cases that have not been predicted correctly can speak back to the process and suggest improvements in theory, measures, and methods" (p. 114).

As a result of the interviews, Pearce was able to refine the prediction model to more accurately predict fertility preferences. Equally important, the information gathered in the interviews allowed her to improve the measurement of key variables in the study. The interviews indicated that some of the respondents either had not understood key questions in the initial survey or had interpreted them in ways vastly different from what was intended.

Another type of sequential mixed-method approach is to start with qualitative techniques and then use quantitative approaches to gain further understanding of the research problem. Richter (1997) studied child-care decision making in Thailand, beginning with a qualitative study of experiences and attitudes about child care. Hypothetical scenarios of women facing child care decisions were presented, and the informants were asked to offer their opinions about the best solution to the situations. A preference model developed from the responses to these scenarios was subsequently tested using data from a representative sample of 1,515 never-married women from the Bangkok metropolitan area. The qualitative data allowed the researchers to better understand the reasoning and motives of mothers making child care decisions and to understand the sequencing of the decision-making process, both of which were not readily discernible from the quantitative data.

Finally, Gomel and her colleagues (1998) conducted a parallel or simultaneous mixed-method study of the effects of economic hardship on family relationships. A total of 285 African American, Euro American, and Latino parents took part in a questionnaire study asking a series of closed-ended questions

concerning the effect of economic recession and its effects on family life—including how the tasks of maintaining a family and home have been altered, how economic distress affects individuals' daily lives, how family relationships and roles are affected, and how family members cope with the situation. (p. 440)

At the same time, a snowball sample of parents of African American, Euro American, and Latino parents was created for a series of focus groups. The probes used in the focus groups covered the same topics under study in the questionnaire study.

The questionnaire data were then used to develop path models predicting objective and perceived economic hardship, the use of individual coping strategies, and changes in family relationships. The focus groups proved to be "a rich source of data for . . . understanding certain microlevel processes involved in the experience of economic hardship among the different groups" (p. 461).

Mixed-Model Studies in Family Research

The third type of designs identified by Tashakkori and Teddlie (1998) are **mixed-model studies,** which "combine the qualitative and quantitative approaches within different phases of the research process" (p. 19) in a number of ways. For example, "a quantitative (experimental) design, followed by qualitative data collection, followed by quantitative analysis after the data are converted" (p. 19) using the *quantitizing* technique suggested by Miles and Huberman (1994).

Other possibilities include simultaneous administration of both closed-ended (for example, Likert-style items) and open-ended questions in the same survey or the simultaneous use of ethnographic interviews and a field experiment in the same project. Smith and his colleagues (1994) wanted to study the reactions of couples and practitioners to the use of reflecting teams in family therapy. They interviewed 11 couples and five therapists at least twice over a four-month period "concerning their reactions to and perceptions of reflecting team practice" (p. 271). All the interviews were recorded on audiotape and transcribed. The interviews were content analyzed and coded within seven categories (for example, "benefits or reasons to have a reflecting team," "specific times when a reflecting team was not useful," and so forth). These categorized data were then analyzed using cross-classification analysis. These analyses suggested that the couples and the therapists stressed different issues about the reflecting team, and that "couples' and therapists' separate worlds of meaning and interpretation result in different appraisals of process and outcome" (p. 280).

Some Closing Thoughts
on Choosing a Research Strategy

When I was a graduate student, the conventional wisdom was that qualitative methods were useful only during the exploratory stage of research (to determine what concepts and processes were important to study). Having used qualitative methods to define the problem, we then used quantitative methods to describe characteristics of the population and test hypotheses about the phenomenon of interest. Today, I think that family researchers are recognizing that the process can just as easily go in the opposite direction: Start with quantitative methods, then proceed to qualitative techniques. More important, researchers are realizing that no single methodological strategy can answer all the questions we might have about families and marriages.

Many methods texts instruct the student to choose the best research strategy for a particular problem, that is, to make the research strategy fit the problem. Although this is good advice, the reality is that no researcher excels in all the strategies mentioned in Chapters 6 and 7. Instead, most researchers specialize in one or perhaps two of these strategies. The researcher's methodological preference often dictates the choice of a research problem rather than the other way around. That is, a researcher trained in large-scale survey methods is unlikely to study problems requiring participant observation, those expert in experimental design are probably not going to choose research problems requiring content analysis, and so forth. Perhaps more important, relatively few researchers trained primarily in quantitative methods conduct qualitative research and vice versa. This is a strong argument for collaborative research by researchers with different types of methodological expertise.

Although we all need to be at least conversant in the major research strategies so we can critically read and evaluate any type of research, the mixed-method approach demands that we take this issue a step further. One barrier to this goal is that "scholars in the mainstream quantitative tradition (the positivists and postpositivists) and qualitative tradition (the constructivists) have not embraced mixed model studies" (Tashakkori & Teddlie, 1998, ix). For example, the *Handbook of Qualitative Research* (Denzin & Lincoln, 1994) has only one chapter that deals with mixed methods, and Cook and Campbell's (1979) classic quantitative text mentioned mixed models only briefly.

We might argue convincingly that the mixed-method approach will come to dominate family research, and not only because no single methodology is likely to be able to answer all of our questions. Creswell (2003) argued that "for the mixed methods researcher, pragmatism opens the door to multiple methods, different worldviews, and different assumptions, as well as to different forms of data collection and analysis" (p. 12). The increasing diversification of family forms—single parenting, cohabiting couples, blended families, and gay, lesbian, bisexual, and transgender couples—suggests the need for alternative strategies of *knowing* about families, marriages, and other intimate relationships.

Study Questions

Develop a family-related research question that interests you and apply it to the following questions.

1. How might you study this research question using a single *quantitative* technique from Chapter 6?

2. How might you study this research question using a single *qualitative* technique from Chapter 7?

3. How might you study this research question with a *mixed-method study* design?

4. How might you study this research question using a *mixed-model study* approach?

5. Finally, how would you evaluate the strengths and weaknesses of each approach for your particular research question?

For Further Reading

Cherryhomes, C. H. (1992). Notes on pragmatism and scientific realism. *Educational Researcher, 14*, 13–17.

Cook, T. D., & Campbell, D. T. (1979). *Quasi-experimentation: Design & analysis issues for field settings.* Boston: Houghton Mifflin.

Creswell, J. W. (2003). *Research design: Qualitative, quantitative, and mixed methods approaches.* Thousand Oaks, CA: Sage.

Denzin, N. K., & Lincoln, Y. S. (Eds.). (1994). *Handbook of qualitative research.* Thousand Oaks, CA: Sage.

Gomel, J. N., Tinsley, B. J., Parke, R. D., & Clark, K. M. (1998). The effects of economic hardship on family relationships among African American, Latino, and Euro American families. *Journal of Family Issues, 19*, 436–467.

Miles, M. B., & Huberman, A. M. (1994). *Qualitative data analysis: An expanded sourcebook* (2nd ed.). Thousand Oaks, CA: Sage.

Pearce, L. D. (2002). Integrating survey and ethnographic methods for systematic anomalous case analysis. *Sociological Methodology, 32*, 102–132.

Richter, K. (1997). Child care choice in urban Thailand—Qualitative and quantitative evidence of the decision-making process. *Journal of Family Issues, 18*, 174–204.

Smith, T. E., Sells, S. P., & Clevenger, T. (1994). Ethnographic content analysis of couple and therapist perceptions in a reflecting team setting. *Journal of Marital and Family Therapy, 20*, 267–286.

Tashakkori, A., & Teddlie, C. (1998). *Mixed methodology: Combining qualitative and quantitative approaches.* Thousand Oaks, CA: Sage.

9

Sampling Issues

S o far, we've discussed how the data are collected. What we haven't talked about is from whom the data are collected. We can't possibly collect data on every single person of interest to us. For example, if we wanted to study children in group day care, we can't possibly observe each of the more than 10 million preschoolers enrolled in group day care centers in the United States today. **Sampling procedures** are the techniques through which we determine which persons or families to observe and how many to observe.

Let's begin by defining some concepts from sampling. The unit about which information is gathered is known as an **element.** Elements and units of analysis are often (but not necessarily) the same in most studies; elements are linked to the sample-selection process, whereas units of analysis refer to the analysis of the data. For example, a researcher sampling households in a given metropolitan area would select specific households to study; the unit of analysis would be the household, and the focus of the analysis would be some aspect of the household—for example, household income or household size. Alternatively, the analysis might focus on characteristics of the married couples in those households (in which case, the unit of analysis would be the couple) or their children (so that the unit of analysis is each individual child).

A **population** is the complete and inclusive collection of all theoretically defined elements. If the population of interest is all children enrolled in group day care, each child enrolled in group day care is an element in that population. A **sample** is the collection of elements drawn from the population that are actually studied. If we decide to study just those children enrolled at Happy Times Childcare, these children constitute the sample under study.

Of course, if you study only the children enrolled at Happy Times Childcare (an expensive child care center located in a wealthy suburb), a critic of your study might (with some justification) argue that your results would have differed had you instead studied the children at Dinoland Day Care (which is located in a disadvantaged section of town). After all, suburban child care centers are likely to charge more, permitting a lower child-to-caregiver ratio and better facilities. In many cases, the research results can be expected to be heavily influenced by who, exactly, is studied.

Sampling procedures help us decide who is studied and how to select those individuals (or households or couples or families or groups or organizations— whichever is our unit of analysis) to produce valid results that can be generalized to the entire population under study. The first step in this process is deciding on the unit of analysis. In Chapter 2, I suggested that family researchers examine data at many units of analysis (e.g., individuals, dyads [couples], coresidential or nuclear families, extended families) and at various levels of aggregation (communities, states, or nations). For research on families and marriages, this is a particularly important issue; and a great deal of thought has to go into deciding on the unit of analysis. If the unit of analysis is the marriage, does that require that we gather data from both spouses? If the unit of analysis is the nuclear family, do we need to collect data on all members of the nuclear family? Or can we rely on the responses of one spouse or one member of the family to provide us with the information we need? If we ask only one spouse, how can we be sure that the information about the other spouse is valid?

Many family researchers (such as Thomson & Williams, 1982; Szinovacz, 1983; Maguire, 1999; Sayer & Klute, 2005) have wrestled with these issues. Let's take an example. Imagine that a researcher wishes to study the effects of family social status on some outcome variable. The unit of analysis here is the family (because we are interested in family social status), but how do we measure this construct? Because husbands tend to have higher-status jobs than their wives, do we look only at the husband's occupational prestige? Do we somehow combine the husband's and wife's occupational-prestige scores in dual-earner marriages? What about single-parent households? What do we do with divorced couples who have joint custody of their children? These are all issues that the researcher must consider when designing the study.

Defining the Population

Thus, a key issue is defining the population of interest. This process has two steps. First, the target population—the population to which we want to generalize our findings—must be defined. To define the target population, we must specify the characteristics that identify the members of the population. Characteristics such as age, income, education, ethnicity, region of residence, and marital status are typically used. For a study of children enrolled in group day care facilities, the target population might be defined as "all children younger than age 6 years who regularly spend at least 30 hours per week in a child care facility that houses a minimum of 60 children."

Next, the **sampling frame** must be constructed. The sampling frame is the set of all elements from which the members of the sample—that is, those persons or groups who will actually be studied—are drawn. The sampling frame is constructed in two ways: Configure (or locate) a list that identifies all the relevant elements, or construct a rule that defines membership in the population. For a telephone interview of the residents of a given city, the local telephone directory is an example of a list that identifies all the residents of a particular area with listed telephone numbers. The set of telephone exchanges (the three-digit prefixes) in a particular area provides a rule. Unless the list is known to be accurate and up-to-date, using a rule to construct the sampling frame is often preferable. For example, we know that the telephone directory is an incomplete list of persons living in a given area. Not all households have telephones, and not all telephone numbers are listed in the telephone directory. These factors are tied to social class: Working-class households are less likely to have telephones, and upper-middle- and upper-class households are more likely to have unlisted numbers or wireless phones that aren't listed in a directory. In addition, the telephone directory is printed only annually, so highly mobile individuals are going to be underrepresented. Another option is to use the three-digit exchanges and then randomly generate the final four digits of the seven-digit number. This removes the bias of unlisted numbers and those whose households are too new to appear in the directory, but it doesn't solve the problem of differential telephone ownership by social class. More detail on telephone survey sampling and procedures can be found in Lavrakas (1993) and in Czaja and Blair (2005).

Ideally, the target population and the sampling frame are identical. In practice, however, this is rarely the case. One problem is that often we want to study persons, families, or groups for whom no lists exist. Moreover, using the rule doesn't identify particular children for study; we still have to go out and find children in the right age group and then determine whether or not they belong in the population of interest. No list exists of "all children younger than age 6 years who regularly spend at least 30 hours per week in a child care facility that houses a minimum of 60 children." We might be able to obtain lists of children in particular child care facilities, however, and use them as a sampling frame (though with the concerns raised earlier). However the sampling frame is constructed, the researcher must be aware of possible biases that might affect the study's results.

Sampling Designs

The next step is to choose a particular sampling technique that will indicate precisely which elements of the sampling frame will be selected for observation (that is, how to select the elements that will be included in the sample). The goal is to obtain a sample whose data will yield results similar to those that would have been obtained if data were collected on the entire population of interest. Sampling designs may be grouped into two broad categories. In **probability sampling,** every member of the target population has a known and nonzero probability of being included in the sample; selection must be random. In **nonprobability sampling,** the probability or likelihood of any given element being included in the sample is unknown.

Probability Samples

Probability sampling offers two crucial advantages over nonprobability sampling. First, because the sampling uses random procedures based on known probabilities of inclusion, the likelihood that the researcher's intentional or inadvertent biases might affect the nature of the sample is reduced. Second, the use of random sampling allows for the use of powerful statistical techniques to estimate the accuracy of the sampling process. Differences between the characteristics of the sample and those of the population are known as **sampling error.** For example, census data (which includes all the households in the metropolitan area) might reveal that 64% of the households in a particular metropolitan area are headed by married couples. Because the population of interest is the set of all households in that metropolitan area, the 64% value represents what is known as a **population parameter**—that is, the actual value of some statistic for the entire population.

In a sample drawn from the population of all households in that metropolitan area, if only 58% of the households are headed by married couples, this 58% value represents the **sample statistic**—the empirical value determined for the elements included in our sample. The difference between the *population parameter* and the *sample statistic* represents the amount of *sampling error* for that particular sample and measurement procedure. Because the probability of including any specific element in the sample is known, researchers can calculate in advance the expected sampling error for any probability sampling procedure. Therefore, probability samples are preferred over nonprobability samples, all things being equal.

In **simple random sampling,** every element in the sampling frame has a known and equal probability of being included in the sample. If a sampling frame contains 1,000 elements, and we are going to draw a sample of 100, the probability of any given element being included in the sample is 100/1,000, or 1/10. Furthermore, we also know the probability of any combination of elements being included in the sample. A key requirement of simple random sampling is that a list or enumeration of every member of the population must exist from which the sample is to be drawn. Because we rarely have a complete list of all the members of a population, simple random samples are not often used in social and behavioral research.

In **stratified random sampling,** the population is divided into **strata** (mutually exclusive segments based on some readily observable characteristic such as zip code, county, or gender). Simple random samples are drawn within each stratum, and these subsamples are combined to form the stratified sample.

As an example, let's say that we want to do a statewide survey on the use of corporal punishment by parents. We know that social class, which is often operationalized as family income, correlates with the use of corporal punishment—parents from higher-social-class families are less likely to use corporal punishment. To ensure that we get a sample of families across a broad range of incomes, we might decide first to classify the counties of the state in terms of median family income (high, medium, low). We then select five counties at random from each of the three groups. Median family income, then, is the stratifying variable in this procedure. We can even have multiple stratifying variables; for example, we might further stratify the counties in terms of how rural they are.

Once the counties have been selected, we can sample families at random within each county. The major advantage of stratified random sampling is that when the stratifying variable is correlated with the key dependent variable in the study the precision of the estimates of the values under study is increased. Under these conditions, a stratified random sample can actually be as precise as a simple random sample of larger size; consequently, stratified random sampling is cost efficient. The drawback to stratified random sampling is that you need to know the values of the stratifying variables before drawing the sample, which is not always possible.

Another advantage of stratified random sampling is that it allows for more precise estimates of values for relatively small groups. In a simple random sample of the population, we find relatively few single-parent households headed by fathers. With a technique called **disproportionate stratified random sampling**, the researcher can obtain a greater proportion of single-father households than occur in the population.

One major drawback of simple random sampling and stratified random sampling is that both require a list of all members of the population. Lists exist of members of various organizations (for example, voters registered with a particular political party), but lists of the general public are unavailable for research purposes. Most government lists of the general public (for example, the decennial census, income tax returns, social security registration) are confidential, and public lists (voter rolls, driver's license lists, telephone directories, city directories) are often selective and quickly become out-of-date.

Cluster sampling may be used when it is difficult or impossible to list the members of the target population. For example, lists of "all children younger than age 6 years who regularly spend at least 30 hours per week in a child care facility that houses a minimum of 60 children" are unavailable, but lists exist of the children enrolled in each facility. In addition, complete lists of all such licensed facilities are available through the state agency responsible for regulation of child care providers. To select which facilities we would study, we might begin by sampling (ideally using a stratified random sample based on the number of children in each of the facilities) from the list of all child care facilities. Then, we could sample within the selected facilities to create our sample.

The major advantages of cluster sampling are that it allows us to draw probability samples even when a list of the target population is unavailable, and its cost is relatively efficient compared to stratified random sampling. The disadvantage is that cluster samples typically have larger sampling errors than stratified random samples of comparable size. Increasing the sample size can offset this drawback (but this, of course, means higher costs). For probability samples, error generally decreases with increasing sample size, but cost increases with sample size. So, researchers are faced with a trade-off between reducing sampling error and reducing costs. Usually, cost is the limiting factor; we know how much money is available to spend gathering data, and we choose our sample size accordingly. More about choosing a sample size later.

Nonprobability Samples

As mentioned earlier, in nonprobability samples, the probability or likelihood of any given element's inclusion in the sample is unknown. Unlike probability samples, nonprobability sampling procedures do not provide control for possible researcher bias in selecting elements for inclusion in the sample, and they offer no means of assessing the amount of sampling error. Despite these drawbacks, nonprobability methods become the preferred alternative in at least four situations where probability sampling is inappropriate, unnecessary, or not feasible.

First, in exploratory or qualitative research, researchers are typically unconcerned with generalizing to a population. In this case, a nonprobability sampling procedure can be adequate. Second, probability sampling is impractical and may even be undesirable when the sample is extremely small. Perhaps the researcher is doing a qualitative study of family dynamics involving intensive observation of families over a period of weeks, thus necessitating a relatively small sample of families. Creating a random sample of size 10 or fewer is not feasible. A similar situation arises when conducting single-case studies, where only one case is of interest. A third situation occurs when the population contains only a few elements. Perhaps you wish to do a comparative study of major American religious denominations and their family-life teachings. This population is relatively small, so studying all the elements in the population, rather than a sample from it, is probably worthwhile. Finally, research is often limited to available data. Data and records might be available on only three nineteenth-century communes in the United States, making any kind of probability sampling meaningless.

Given these situations, four major types of nonprobability sampling procedures might be employed: convenience sampling, quota sampling, purposive sampling, and snowball sampling.

As its name suggests, **convenience samples** are composed of those elements that are convenient for the researcher to study. As an example, suppose we wanted to study preschoolers' reactions to strangers. We might get the permission of a local day care center to study the reactions of the children enrolled there to strangers in a controlled situation. Although the results of the study might be interesting and informative, the problem with the convenience sample is that it's never clear to what population (if any) the findings might apply. And, as in all nonprobability techniques, estimating the amount of sampling error (or the value of a population parameter) involved in the procedure is impossible. Most often, convenience samples are used during the exploratory stages of research.

In **purposive sampling**, researchers deliberately attempt to select cases that, in their professional judgment, represent the population of interest. Specific cases are selected precisely because they are believed to be typical. In the reactions-to-strangers study mentioned previously, a researcher might deliberately select one day care center in a suburban area, another in a rural area, and a third in an inner city to study differences in reactions to strangers by children from different types of residential areas. Although purposive sampling may appear to be more scientifically valid than convenience sampling, it is heavily dependent on a comprehensive understanding of the processes under study by the researcher.

Quota sampling involves creating a sample whose characteristics mirror those of some population of interest. Because it is difficult to draw a probability sample of preschoolers, the researcher might instead opt for a quota sample. As in a stratified random sample, the researcher begins by dividing the population of interest into relevant strata such as ethnicity and family income. Then the proportion of the population that falls into each category of the stratifying variables (for example, the percentage of families who are below the poverty line) is determined. The goal is to create a sample with the same percentage of preschoolers from families below the poverty line as occur in the population.

Unlike stratified random sampling, however, quota samples do not select cases randomly; instead, the cases can be selected through any method that the researcher finds feasible. One way to think about a quota sample is to realize that it is really a convenience sample whose composition matches the population along the dimensions of the stratifying variables.

Snowball sampling is often used to study groups or individuals that are hard to identify or locate. Risman and Johnson-Sumerford (1998) wanted to study issues relating to the division of household labor in dual-career couples that shared household tasks evenly. Because such couples constitute only a tiny fraction of all married couples and because they are unlisted, the researchers built their sample by asking each couple that met their criteria to suggest other such couples that might fit the study's requirements. In this sense, the continuing growth of their sample resembled a snowball rolling down a hill, increasing in size as it picks up more snow in its path. One drawback of snowball samples is the fact that because members of a snowball sample know each other, there is the possibility for potential bias in the sample.

How Large Does the Sample Need to Be?

A common question raised by readers of family research has to do with sample size. How small a sample is too small? How can we determine whether a sample is sufficiently large? For simple random samples, the process of determining sample size is relatively straightforward. Generally speaking, determination of sample size boils down to three major considerations: the amount of sampling error that can be tolerated, the amount of variability in the dependent variable, and the cost of gathering data about additional observations. As sample size increases, the amount of sampling error decreases (which is good); but as sample size increases, so does cost (which is bad). Researchers, therefore, are faced with a trade-off: They can draw large samples with relatively small amounts of sampling error but at a high cost; or they can draw smaller samples that cost less but have relatively higher amounts of sampling error. Cohen (1988) presented a detailed introduction to sample-size determination. For simple random samples, if the amount of sampling error can be determined (or estimated), a simple equation can be used to calculate required sample size.

Here is one basis for comparison: Most national samples of 1,000 to 1,500 cases have sampling error amounts in the plus-or-minus 3% to 4% range. This means we can be relatively confident that the population values—that is, the response we would have obtained had we the resources to collect data on all the members of the sample population—are within 3% to 4% of the sample estimates. Sampling-error and sample-size determination for large national samples are complicated by the fact that such surveys almost never use simple random samples; they are more likely to use some type of multi-level combination of stratified random and cluster sampling. Of course, given the absence of any practical way to estimate sampling error for nonprobability samples, these rules apply only to probability samples.

How Do We Go About Choosing a Sampling Technique?

Given their shortcomings, you might wonder why anyone would use nonprobability samples. Ideally, every research project should use a large, stratified random sample with relatively small sampling errors that render the findings of the study readily generalizable to the population of interest. In reality, however, pragmatic considerations often make it difficult for researchers to work with such samples. Much research is conducted directly by individual researchers without additional assistance, making it impractical to build large samples. The costs of doing stratified random samples make them nearly impossible to use without substantial funding from government agencies or private foundations. And certain kinds of research strategies— in-depth interviews, participant observation, and most qualitative studies, for example—don't lend themselves well to probability sampling.

As a result of these factors, too many nonprobability samples are in the family research literature. Although the findings of these studies may not be readily generalizable to any particular population, they still may be of great value in understanding how social processes operate, especially on topics where relatively little research has been conducted or theory is poorly developed.

Study Questions

1. Find a published report in a newspaper or magazine of a public opinion poll. What information is given about how the sample of respondents was selected? What information do you need to judge the representativity of the sampling procedure?

2. Choose three quantitative research studies on families from professional journals that use different sampling procedures. For each study, identify (a) the population, (b) the type of sampling procedure, and (c) the unit of analysis. For each study, consider whether the sampling procedure appears to be representative of the population.

3. Give examples of three different populations (for example, the set of all registered sex offenders in New Hampshire) that could be readily sampled using a simple random sampling procedure or other type of probability sampling. Then, give examples of three different populations (for example, the set of all persons who have nightmares about sharks) that most likely could not be sampled using probability procedures, and suggest a possible nonprobability sampling procedure for each case.

For Further Reading

Cohen, J. (1988). *Statistical power analysis for the behavioral sciences* (2nd ed.). Hillsdale, NJ: Erlbaum.

Czaja, R., & Blair, J. (2005). *Designing surveys: A guide to decisions and procedures* (2nd ed.). Thousand Oaks, CA: Pine Forge.

Lavrakas, P. J. (1993). *Telephone survey methods: Sampling, selection, and supervision* (2nd ed.). Newbury Park, CA: Sage.

Maguire, M. C. (1999). Treating the dyad as the unit of analysis: A primer on three analytic approaches. *Journal of Marriage and the Family, 61*, 213–223.

Risman, B. J., & Johnson-Sumerford, D. (1998). Doing it fairly: A study of postgender marriages. *Journal of Marriage and the Family, 60*, 23–40.

Sayer, A. G., & Klute, M. M. (2005). Analyzing couples and families: Multilevel methods. In V. L. Bengtson, A. C. Acock, K. R. Allen, P. Dilworth-Anderson, & D. M. Klein (Eds.), *Sourcebook of family theory and research* (pp. 289–313). Thousand Oaks, CA: Sage.

Szinovacz, M. E. (1983). Using couple data as a methodological tool: The case of marital violence. *Journal of Marriage and the Family, 45*, 633–644.

Thomson, E., & Williams, R. (1982). Beyond wives' family sociology: A method for analyzing couple data. *Journal of Marriage and the Family, 44*, 999–1008.

10

Working With Scales and Indices

S ome concepts can be easily measured using a single questionnaire item. Marital status, for example, is typically measured with a single item. Other concepts or constructs—particularly those measuring attitudes, psychological traits, or complex behaviors—require multiple questionnaire items to be operationalized in a meaningful way.

There are two reasons why a specific concept might require more than one questionnaire item to be operationalized in a valid fashion. Consider the measurement of marital satisfaction. Most researchers agree that the construct of marital satisfaction is probably **multidimensional**—that is, there are multiple aspects or dimensions of marital satisfaction that are interrelated yet distinct. For example, we might think of how satisfied married persons are with their marital sex lives; how satisfied they are with how well they communicate with their spouses; how satisfied they are with the allocation of power in their marriages; and so on. People who are satisfied with their sex lives might not be satisfied with the allocation of power; those who are satisfied with the quality of communication might not be too happy about their sex lives. Clearly, a valid and reliable measure of marital satisfaction is going to require several questionnaire items to tap these multiple dimensions.

A second reason that multiple questionnaire items might be necessary to measure a single concept is that multiple items are often necessary to create an ordinal measure of the concept. For example, a researcher studying the behavior of dating couples might require an ordinal measure of physical intimacy. Level of physical intimacy might range from no physical contact at all to frequent sexual intercourse, with many levels in between—holding hands, kissing, fondling, and petting. To measure this concept, the researcher might include a series of questionnaire items about each form of intimate behavior. Note that the concept of physical intimacy is probably **unidimensional**—a single continuum or dimension of sexual intimacy, ranging from least to most intimate.

Scales and indices are the two primary techniques that social scientists employ for handling concepts and constructs that must be measured with multiple items. Babbie (2004) suggests that although they appear to be similar, scales and indices are two different kinds of composite measures (pp. 162–163). An **index** is the result of the simple accumulation of scores to measure the extent or quantity of some attribute. An index of the level of conflict in a marriage, for example, might use multiple questionnaire items to ascertain the level or degree of conflict. A simple index might simply add up the number of *yes* responses to questions about whether the couple argues about various issues in their marriage. Such an index, however, implicitly assumes that each of the conflict areas is of roughly equal importance. Standardized tests such as the Scholastic Assessment Test (SAT) or intelligence quotient (IQ) tests are indices; their scores reflect the extent to which the respondent could correctly answer the questions in the test.

A **scale,** however, is intended to reflect a pattern of responses and can include aspects of the intensity of beliefs or behaviors that may exist. Scales also can take into account the possibility that some beliefs or behaviors are more important or more consequential than others. In the literature on families and children, there are three major types of scales: Guttman scaling, semantic differential, and Likert scales.

Types of Scales and Indices

Guttman scaling, introduced by sociologist Louis Guttman (1950), is based on the notion that attitudes and other concepts may be measured as hierarchical structures. Consider our example of the concept of level of physical intimacy in dating couples. We conceptualize level of physical intimacy as a dimension or continuum ranging from least intimate to most intimate. At the least intimate end of the continuum, we might think in terms of whether a couple holds hands; we might place having sexual intercourse at the most intimate end of the continuum. Between these extremes there are a range of other behaviors: hugging, kissing, fondling, and so forth.

The idea underlying Guttman scaling, as applied to our example, is that if these different types of behaviors really comprise a scale, couples who report the highest level of physical intimacy (sexual intercourse) are likely to be engaging in all or most of the less intimate behaviors as well. Those who report that they are not having sexual intercourse but fondle are probably kissing and hugging and so forth. Diagrammatically, the response patterns might look like the depiction in Table 10.1.

Table 10.1   Response Patterns for a *Perfect* Guttman Scale

Level of Intimacy	*Response Pattern*				
Holding hands	Yes	Yes	Yes	Yes	Yes
Hugging	No	Yes	Yes	Yes	Yes
Kissing	No	No	Yes	Yes	Yes
Fondling, petting	No	No	No	Yes	Yes
Sexual intercourse	No	No	No	No	Yes
Scale score	1	2	3	4	5

Table 10.2   Semantic Differential Scale Measuring Attitude Toward Housework

Interesting	1	2	3	4	5	6	7	8	9	Boring
Appreciated	1	2	3	4	5	6	7	8	9	Ignored
Valuable	1	2	3	4	5	6	7	8	9	Worthless
Important	1	2	3	4	5	6	7	8	9	Unimportant

A couple with the highest level of physical intimacy would report engaging in all five of the behaviors and receive a scale score of 5; those engaging in only the lowest level of physical intimacy—holding hands—would receive a score of 1. (You could also argue that there should be a scale score of zero for those who didn't answer *yes* to any of the items.) One interesting quality of a Guttman scale is that the scale score reveals exactly where the respondent stands on the continuum being measured: A couple with a score of 2, for example, hugs and holds hands but doesn't kiss, fondle, or have intercourse. Guttman scales are clearly *ordinal*—each score on the scale represents a higher level of intimacy than any lower score—but not *interval,* because the meanings of the intervals between scale scores can be inconsistent. Hampe and Ruppel (1974) offered an interesting discussion of two different Guttman scales measuring sexual permissiveness.

Semantic differential scales assume that respondents can locate their feelings or attitudes along a series of bipolar dimensions—that is, along several dimensions of extremes, such as valuable to worthless or appreciated to ignored. We might ask married persons how they feel about the housework that they do by indicating, as depicted in Table 10.2, the approximate number on the scale that corresponds to their feelings. A respondent who felt that her housework was appreciated by her family may circle 1 or 2, whereas one who felt that housework was ignored might circle 8 or 9.

One of the advantages of the semantic differential technique is that it allows the respondent's feelings about a concept—housework, in the preceding example—to exist along multiple dimensions simultaneously. Respondents can feel that their housework is appreciated but boring, for example. A full discussion of interpretation and use of semantic differential scales is beyond the scope of this text (the classic treatment is presented by Osgood, Suci, & Tannenbaum, 1957), but a variety of different analytic techniques may be applied to semantic differential data in the search for the underlying dimensions of feelings about the concept under study.

Table 10.3   Likert Scale to Measure Attitudes Toward the Employment of Mothers

	Response Choice				
Question	Strongly Disagree	Disagree Somewhat	Unsure	Agree Somewhat	Strongly Agree
1. Employed mothers can create as warm and loving a relationship with their children as mothers who stay at home.	1	2	3	4	5
2. Preschool children are harmed by having an employed mother.	1	2	3	4	5
3. Children cared for outside the home are at greater risk of becoming delinquent.	1	2	3	4	5
4. Having an employed mother provides a positive role model for children.	1	2	3	4	5

Likert scales are probably the most frequently used format for questionnaire items, especially those dealing with attitudes and opinions. When the response choices are similar to *strongly agree, agree somewhat, unsure, disagree somewhat,* and *strongly disagree,* the response categories are clearly ordinal in nature. Some researchers argue that individual Likert-style items can be treated as interval-level data, but this position is not universally held.

The response choices in Likert-style items are typically given arbitrary numerical values for analytic purposes. The strongly agree category might be coded as 5, agree somewhat as 4, through strongly disagree as 1. For example, to measure attitudes toward the employment of mothers of young children, we might present the items shown in Table 10.3.

The responses to a series of Likert-style items are often summed together to produce a scale score. To reduce the problems of acquiescence bias, some of the items in the scale are usually reversed. Notice that agreeing with items #1 and #4 indicates a positive attitude toward employed mothers, but agreeing with items #2 and #3 indicates a negative attitude toward employed mothers. When summing the scale scores, items #2 and #4 are reversed (strongly agree responses are coded 1, agree-somewhat responses are coded 2, and so forth) to produce a scale in which higher total scores means more favorable attitudes toward employed mothers. I used a Likert-style scale of gender ideology—that is, beliefs about men's and women's roles in families—in my 1996 study (Greenstein, 1996) of inequalities in the division of household labor and marital quality.

Using Existing Scales and Indices

Because so much research is being done that involves studying families and children, many scales, indices, and other measuring instruments have already been developed and tested by researchers. Most of these instruments are in the public domain, and many of the copyrighted instruments are available for use with permission of the original author. Why go to the trouble of creating your own scale when other researchers have already done so?

Where to Find Them

There are two outstanding sourcebooks of existing scales and indices for use in research on families and children. The *Handbook of Family Measurement Techniques* (Touliatos, Perlmutter, Strauss, & Holden, 2001)—indexed by author, title, and subject—includes descriptions and source information for more than 1,000 instruments that measure marriage and family concepts. *Measures of Personality and Social Psychological Attitudes* (Robinson, Shaver, & Wrightsman, 1991) provides descriptions and source information on more general social-psychological measures.

Permission, Copyrights, and So Forth

It's important to remember that many published scales, indices, and questionnaire items are copyrighted materials. Although a few scales are commercially produced and the owners require payment for their reproduction, many researchers will gladly give you permission to use their materials for research purposes at no charge, as long as you acknowledge the source of the materials. Write the authors at their home institutions (as given in the published materials) to request permission, briefly outlining your proposed research. It's wise to keep the permission letter in your files in case a question arises at some future date.

How Do We Evaluate Scales and Indices?

All the issues regarding validity and reliability discussed in Chapter 3 apply to scales and indices as well as to individual items. Clearly, we want our scales and indices to be both reliable (stable over time) and valid (actually measure what they are intended to measure). Besides these concerns, however, is a problem with multiple-item scales and indices: Many of the underlying constructs that family researchers measure with scales and indices are multidimensional.

Dimensionality

Earlier in this chapter, I discussed the concept of marital satisfaction and how it probably has multiple dimensions or aspects that are distinct yet almost certainly correlated with each other. Now, if marital satisfaction really is multidimensional, the scale or index measuring this concept should tap these multiple dimensions. But we have to respect this multidimensionality when we construct and use the scale; we can't simply add up a series of questionnaire items that tap multiple dimensions of marital satisfaction. This is the problem of **internal consistency** (or internal reliability).

Determining Internal Consistency of Scales and Indices

To determine if a scale or index is multidimensional, two simple statistics often reported are the **split-half reliability** and **Cronbach's α** (alpha) coefficient. Alpha is the more general measure, but both range from 0 to 1 and are interpreted in basically the same way: High values (that is, values close to one) indicate high levels of internal consistency, and suggest that all or most of the items in the scale are measuring the same underlying concept. Low values, however, suggest that not all the items are measuring the same concept. Typically, alpha values more than .70 or so are considered to indicate relatively good internal reliability, whereas values much less than .70 suggest that the scale is probably multidimensional and might better be treated as having more than one underlying concept.

Factor analysis is often used to study the dimensional nature of scales and indices. Factor analytic techniques (Jackson & Borgatta, 1981; Long, 1983) can be used in an exploratory mode, to uncover the structure of concepts, or in a confirmatory mode, to study how well some predefined structure fits empirical data. Exploratory factor analysis can be used to examine which items in a scale seem to hang together in clusters or factors, suggesting underlying dimensions to the concept under study.

How Do We Deal With
Missing Data in Scales and Indices?

A common problem encountered by researchers working with multiple-item scales and indices is that of **missing data.** Often, a respondent will answer some but not all the items in a scale. Construction of a scale score is usually dependent on the respondent having provided codable (that is, nonmissing) responses to all the items in the scale. How do researchers typically deal with this problem?

The first issue to consider when dealing with missing data is why the respondent failed to respond to a particular item or items. Respondents find some kinds of questions—for example, those dealing with income, sex, or drug use—too personal to answer in a questionnaire or interview. Other questions might not be answered because the respondent didn't understand the wording. A key issue in the treatment of missing data has to do with the respondent's motives and the relationship of nonresponse to other factors. In some cases, no other variables predict whether a respondent will provide a codable response to a particular item. This pattern is known as *missing completely at random*: the missing data do not represent any particular pattern, and every individual has the same likelihood of being a nonrespondent.

Often, however, the pattern of missing responses is related to some other variable or variables. Those with high income levels seem to be less likely to respond to questions about earnings; those engaging in unlawful activities (for example, drug use or domestic violence) seem to be less likely to respond to questions about those activities. In this pattern, known as *missing at random,* nonresponse is a function of some characteristic of the respondent.

If the data are truly missing completely at random, the missing data don't present much of a problem for analysis, because the respondents who provided complete information are probably representative of the entire population. However, a systematic bias in the pattern of missing data can create serious problems for interpretation. Unfortunately, the pattern of missing data is often not random. Married persons who don't respond to an item about their spouse's income may not know the actual value because the couple is separated. Noncustodial parents who don't answer questions about their children may refuse to answer because of hostility surrounding the custody decision or because they are not involved with their children's lives. Persons undergoing marital conflict may not respond to questions about their family lives, and individuals who are cohabiting with an unmarried partner may indicate in an interview that they live alone. In each of these cases, failure to respond to the questionnaire item suggests a systematic bias in the response pattern.

Strategies for Dealing With Missing Data

One way of dealing with missing data is to simply eliminate from the working or analytic sample any respondent who doesn't provide codable responses to all the items in the analyses. This technique is known as **listwise deletion,** but it has at least two major drawbacks. First, if the data are not missing completely at random, the potential for bias in the working or analytic sample is enormous. It seems unreasonable to expect that those respondents who faithfully answered every single item in our questionnaire are exactly like those who failed to respond to at least one item. Researchers who use listwise deletion will generally perform auxiliary analyses to show that such bias, if present, does not change the substantive interpretation of the analyses.

Another, less common strategy of dealing with missing data is called **pairwise deletion,** in which a respondent is eliminated only from those analyses for which he or she provides a noncodable response. The problem here is that the size of the working or analytic sample can change from analysis to analysis, and it's never clear exactly which collection of respondents is being studied.

As a general rule of thumb, listwise deletion is the preferable technique, especially if the rate of missing data is relatively low (say, fewer than 10%). Missing data rates much higher than 10% require the researcher to show why the missing data do not present a problem for interpretation and generalization of findings.

High rates of missing data may suggest exploring other possible avenues, as well. **Means substitution** is one technique often seen in the literature. It assumes that the best estimate or guess for the value of the response that would have been made, had the respondent answered the question, is the overall mean value for that variable in the sample. For example, if a respondent didn't answer our question on number of years of education, we might substitute the mean value for years of education for that sample (based on those respondents who did answer the question). This is probably a reasonable strategy if the data for the education item are missing completely at random, but any systematic bias in the nonresponse patterns means substitution may produce misleading results.

Occasionally, researchers will use other statistical techniques to impute missing values. For example, a researcher may decide to impute a value for income, for those respondents who didn't answer the question, by basing a guess or imputation for income on the respondent's educational level. In some cases, several variables might be combined to produce such imputed values.

Despite the availability of these techniques, however, the fundamental question presented by missing data—especially when there are large amounts of it—has to do with the underlying source of the problem. *Why* are respondents failing to answer particular questions? If the missing responses are not systematic—that is, if the failure to respond to a particular item is not associated with some other characteristic of the respondent, such as age, ethnicity, income, or education—then the missing data do not usually represent a major problem. However, high rates of nonresponse raise serious questions of questionnaire design and survey administration that probably can't be resolved purely by statistical means. Mailed questionnaires are likely to have the highest rates of missing data; with better questionnaire design and the use of follow-up questions and probes, telephone or personal interviews can usually keep the amount of missing data to an acceptable level. Little and Rubin (1989) give a thorough, but technical, presentation on the problems of missing data.

Study Questions

1. Locate an example of an original (that is, one that hasn't appeared in previously published work) Guttman, Likert, or semantic differential scale or index in any of the major journals that publish research on families. Reproduce the scale items in your answer. What kinds of reliability and validity data do the authors report for the scale? Is the scale unidimensional or multidimensional? How do you know?

2. Find a published scale or index measuring some family-related concept in either of the two sourcebooks mentioned in this chapter. Then find two articles in any of the major family journals that use that scale or index. For each article, report whether the authors use the scale or index as it was published or made modifications to the scale.

3. Think of two questions to which respondents might be likely to fail to respond in a mailed questionnaire. For each of the variables, discuss whether such nonresponse is likely to be random or systematic. If you think that the nonresponse is likely to be systematic, with what variable or variables would it be associated?

For Further Reading

Babbie, E. (2004). *The practice of social research* (10th ed.). Belmont, CA: Wadsworth.

Greenstein, T. N. (1996). Gender ideology and perceptions of the fairness of the division of household labor: Effects on marital quality. *Social Forces, 74,* 1029–1042.

Guttman, L. (1950). The basis for scalogram analysis. In L. G. S. A. Stouffer, E. A. Suchman, P. F. Lazarsfeld, S. A. Star, & J. A. Clausen (Eds.), *Measurement and prediction* (pp. 60–90). Princeton, NJ: Princeton University Press.

Hampe, G. D., & Ruppel, H. J. (1974). Measurement of premarital sexual permissiveness—Comparison of 2 Guttman scales. *Journal of Marriage and the Family, 36,* 451–463.

Jackson, D. J., & Borgatta, E. F. (1981). *Factor analysis and measurement in sociological research: A multi-dimensional perspective.* London: Sage.

Little, R. J. A., & Rubin, D. B. (1989). The analysis of social science data with missing values. *Sociological Methods and Social Research, 18,* 292–326.

Long, J. S. (1983). *Confirmatory factor analysis: A preface for LISREL.* Beverly Hills, CA: Sage.

Osgood, C. E., Suci, C. J., & Tannenbaum, P. H. (1957). *The measurement of meaning.* Urbana: University of Illinois Press.

Robinson, J. P., Shaver, P. R., & Wrightsman, L. S. (1991). *Measures of personality and social psychological attitudes.* San Diego: Academic Press.

Touliatos, J., Perlmutter, B. F., Strauss, M. A., & Holden, G. W. (2001). *Handbook of family measurement techniques* (2nd ed.). Thousand Oaks, CA: Sage.

11

Analyzing Data on Families

A rticles and monographs studying families and children overwhelmingly report some type of statistical tests or measures, what are sometimes called **quantitative analysis.** Although the language of statistical analysis may seem a bit daunting at first, the good news is that you can develop a basic ability to interpret the results of common statistical techniques fairly easily.

Statistical techniques can be grouped into two general categories. **Descriptive statistics** are techniques used to summarize information about samples. **Inferential statistics** are used to make statements about population characteristics based on sample data.

Descriptive Statistics

Descriptive statistics allow us to summarize data gathered from large numbers of respondents. If you are studying only a few families, you could easily summarize the characteristics of those families in a paragraph or two. You could talk about their general neighborhoods, the parents' jobs, the number of children in each family, and so forth. This becomes impossible, however, if you're looking at more than a handful of respondents. Just listing the occupations of 400 sets of parents takes up several sheets of paper, which makes it difficult to get a grasp of the general patterns.

Descriptive statistics are designed to summarize the numerical distribution of sample data. We are generally concerned with three aspects of our sample distributions. **Central tendency** measures look at the location of our data: Where on the continuum are most respondents' scores located? Do they tend to have high-, low-, or middle-range scores? Second, we are concerned with the dispersion of the data. Measures of **variability** indicate how widespread or dispersed the data are across the continuum. Are most respondents' scores concentrated at one or two points along the continuum? Or are the scores somewhat evenly scattered? Finally, **measures of association** tell us how two or more variables are related to each other in the sample data.

Measures of Central Tendency

The most commonly reported measure of central tendency is the **mean** score, which is simply the numerical average of the scores. The mean is only appropriate for use with variables at the interval or ratio level of measurement.

Another common measure of central tendency is the **median** (also referred to as the 50th percentile), which is the score that divides the sample distribution in half. Half of the respondents' scores are above the median, and half of the respondents' scores are below the median. When government reports say that the median family income in the United States is $38,200, this means that half of all families have incomes below $38,200 and half have incomes above that level. The median is appropriate for data measured at the ordinal, interval, or ratio levels.

Finally, the **mode** is the most frequently appearing score in the sample distribution. It is appropriate for variables at all levels of measurement.

When discussing central tendency of an interval- or ratio-level variable, family researchers will usually report only the mean for a variable unless the distribution of the variable is highly skewed one way or another. Family income is a good example of a variable with a highly skewed distribution; although most households are clustered in the lower end of the distribution, a few households are far out on the high end of the income range—which tends to pull the estimate of the mean value upward.

For example, in 2003, the U.S. Census Bureau reported that the mean or average income of American households was $59,067 (DeNavas-Walt, Proctor, & Mills, 2004). This figure is misleading, however, because the distribution of household income is skewed or lopsided—there are far more households at the low end of the distribution than at the high end. However, a relatively small number of households with extremely high incomes can *pull* the mean upward. In fact, the median household income in 2003 was $43,318. In other words, even though the average or mean household income was $59,067, 50% of all American households reported less than $43,318 in income (in fact, nearly 30% reported less than $25,000 in income).

Measures of Variability

Probably the most frequently used measure of central tendency is the **standard deviation,** which measures the amount of variability in variables measured at the interval or ratio levels. Smaller values of the standard deviation indicate less variability in the scores, whereas larger values suggest more variability. A standard deviation of 0 means that all the scores are at the same point or value in the distribution; in other words, there is no variability in the distribution. The **variance** is the value of the standard deviation squared. Both the variance and standard deviation are appropriate only for data measured at the interval or ratio levels.

The **range** is simply the arithmetic difference between the lowest and highest scores in the distribution. For example, if the smallest household in a data set has only 1 member and the largest has 17 members, the range is $17 - 1$, or 16. The **interquartile range** is the difference between the first-quartile score (below which 25% of the scores fall) and the third-quartile score (below which 75% of the scores fall).

Let's illustrate these terms with a concrete example. Wave 1 of the National Survey of Families and Households surveyed 13,017 adults in the United States during 1987. The household incomes ranged from $0 to $988,672, yielding a range of 988,672. The first-quartile score was $6,000 (meaning that 25% of the households had total incomes of $6,000 or less), and the third-quartile score was $36,000, giving an interquartile range of $30,000. The mean or average total household income was $26,034, and the median household income was $18,000. The mode, or the most frequently reported income level, was $0. The standard deviation for the household-income data was $37,212, and the variance was $1,384,780,895.

Measures of Association

Family researchers often need to know how variables are related to (or associated with) each other. Is wives' income related to the probability of divorce? How are spouses' educational levels and frequency of marital violence associated? Are parental cognitive-ability levels related to the ability levels of children?

The choice of a specific **measure of association** is largely dependent on the level of measurement for the variables involved. When the variables are measured at the nominal level, commonly reported measures are **lambda** (λ_{yx}) and the **uncertainty coefficient** (U_{yx}). Each takes on values between 0 and 1, where 1 indicates a **perfect relationship**—that is, knowing the value of the independent variable allows you to perfectly predict the value of the dependent variable—and 0 indicates no relationship at all. Notice that these measures do not connote direction of the relationship, because it doesn't make sense to speak of the direction of a relationship between two nominally scaled variables (that is, we can't say that there is a positive or negative relationship between marital status and income; we can merely assert that some marital statuses have higher mean incomes than others).

For ordinal-level data, the measures of choice are usually **gamma** (γ) or **Somer's D_{yx}**. They range from –1 (indicating a perfect negative relationship) through zero (indicating no relationship) to +1 (indicating a perfect positive relationship). When working with ordinally scaled variables, the direction of the relationship is important and meaningful. That is, it makes sense to say that there is a positive association between mother's cognitive skills and those of her children.

The **correlation coefficient** (often referred to as Pearson's r) is the most commonly used measure of association for interval-level data. The correlation coefficient also ranges from –1 through zero to +1. The **coefficient of determination** (often referred to as r^2) is the square of the correlation coefficient and ranges from 0 to +1.

When interpreting measures of association, it's important to remember that there are no perfect associations in real-world data. Correlation coefficient values of .1 or .2 are common in analyses of data on families, and the failure to attain values close to 1 should not necessarily be taken as an indication that the relationship or association is not substantively important. As with most things in social research, we need to consider the values of the measures of association in the context of the research topic and especially in comparison to findings from similar studies.

Interpreting Cross-classification Tables

Research findings involving categorical variables are often reported in the form of **cross-classification tables.** The construction of such tables is relatively straightforward. They consist of a series of rows (usually representing the categories of the dependent variable) and columns (usually representing the categories of the independent variable) that intersect to form a series of cells. The entries in the cells usually represent the number of observations in the sample that fall into that combination of values of the independent and dependent variables. Another value that might appear in the cells represents the percentage of respondents within a particular category of the independent variable who also possessed a particular category of the dependent variable.

Table 11.1 is an example of a cross-classification table. Notice that the table has a descriptive title ("Effects of Marital Status on General Happiness") that identifies the independent (marital status) and dependent (general happiness) variables. The source of the data, the General Social Survey (a national sample of American adults interviewed in 2002), is given beneath the table. The rows of the table represent the categories of the dependent variable (happiness): *very happy, pretty happy,* and *not too happy.* The columns of the table represent the categories of the independent variable (marital status): *currently married, separated, divorced, widowed,* and *never married.*

In each cell in the table are two numbers. Examine the cell for persons who are married and very happy (the upper-left cell in the table). The cell entries inform us that there were 247 such people out of the 1,369 respondents. These 247 married people who said that they were "very happy" make up 40.9% of the 604 currently married people in the sample. Put another way, the table tells us that of the currently married people in our sample, in addition to the 40.9% very happy people, 52.8% said that they were "pretty happy," and only 6.3% said that they were "not too happy."

If we compare the figures with those of never-married individuals, an interesting picture emerges. Married people are about one and a half times as likely as those who have never been married to be very happy: More than

Table 11.1   Effects of Marital Status on General Happiness

| | Marital Status | | | | | |
Happiness	Currently Married	Separated	Divorced	Widowed	Never Married	Totals
Very happy	247 (40.9%)	70 (25.2%)	34 (15.9%)	28 (22.2%)	97 (26.0%)	415
Pretty happy	319 (52.8%)	149 (53.6%)	138 (64.5%)	77 (61.1%)	419 (57.9%)	784
Not too happy	38 (6.3%)	59 (21.2%)	42 (19.6%)	21 (16.7%)	99 (16.1%)	170
Totals	604 (100%)	52 (100%)	214 (100%)	126 (100%)	373 (100%)	1,369 (100%)

Source: General Social Survey, 2002

Note: Table entries are cell frequencies and, in parentheses, column percentages.

40% of the married people said that they were very happy, whereas only 26% of the *never marrieds* felt this way. And whereas only about 6% of the married persons said that they were not too happy, more than 16% of the never marrieds fell into this category.

The general strategy for interpreting cross-classification tables, therefore, is fairly straightforward. If the table is set up properly (with the categories of the independent variable represented in the columns of the table and the categories of the dependent variable in the rows) and the percentages are calculated correctly (within categories of the independent variable), we can compare percentages within categories of the dependent variable across categories of the independent variable.

Interpreting this table, we can conclude that married persons are more likely to say that they are very happy and less likely to say that they are not too happy than are persons of any other marital status. In other words, it looks as if marital status is associated with general happiness: Married people tend to be happier than those who are separated, divorced, widowed, or never married.

A logical next step is to calculate the appropriate measure of association (for this particular table, the uncertainty coefficient would be a good choice) to measure the strength of the association between marital status and general happiness. The uncertainty coefficient for these data is .043. Although this value is not particularly large (recall that the uncertainty coefficient ranges from 0 to 1), in the context of the research problem, a result of .043 is about in the range of what a researcher would expect to find for these two variables. Any conclusions about the existence of an association, however, require what is known as an inferential test.

Inferential Statistics

The purpose of descriptive statistics is to describe the characteristics of a sample. Typically, however, we are not primarily concerned with the characteristics of the respondents in the sample; we are more interested in knowing something about the characteristics of the population from which the sample data were drawn. For example, it's nice to know the value of the median family size in a particular sample of families, but the value of the median family size in the entire population from which the sample was drawn probably is more interesting.

Inferential statistics are designed to make inferences or estimates about the population values of measures of central tendency, variation, or association based on sample data. Inferential statistics use the characteristics of probability samples to make estimates about the likelihood or probability that a particular population parameter is equal to a particular value or within a particular range of values. Whenever authors write about significance levels or probability levels, they are almost certainly using inferential statistics to make estimates of population values.

There are at least two different uses of the term *significance* in the research literature. One has to do with **substantive significance.** Simply put, substantive significance asks, "Is this a difference that really matters?" If the median family size for one group is 3.32 persons and the median for another group is 3.14 persons, the two groups have *different* median family sizes. But is this a large enough difference to make a difference? That is, do any theoretical, social, or policy implications result from this difference of .18 persons? This type of question can be answered only in the context of the research question. In some areas of research, a difference of .18 might be important indeed; in others, it may be trivial.

Statistical significance, however, refers to the results of inferential tests. In their most general form, tests of statistical significance ask, "How likely is this (or a more extreme) result to have occurred by chance?" The conventional standard for statistical significance is the .05 (or 5%) level, suggesting that such a result occurs only 5% of the time by chance alone. Inferential tests with results at or beyond this level (that is, probability levels equal to or less than .05) generally indicate real effects or differences in the populations from which the data were drawn. An author might write that a particular difference is "statistically significant beyond the .05 level," meaning that that the probability associated with the inferential test was .05 or less.

Another way of thinking about statistical significance is in terms of inferences about populations. Analyses of sample data are often used to make inferences about the populations from which the samples were drawn. When researchers perform significance tests on sample data, they are attempting to test hypotheses about the population based on the sample data. For example, we might want to compare income levels for 900 husbands and wives from a national sample of married persons. In the sample, the mean (average) income for husbands might be $6,000 more than the mean income for wives. In other words, the mean income levels for husbands and wives in this sample are, without question, different; the differential between the two groups is $6,000. However, we are less concerned about these particular 900 husbands and wives than we are with what these sample data can tell us about the total population of husbands and wives in the United States (about 70 million at last count). Consequently, the sample data might be used to test the hypothesis that, in the population from which the sample data were drawn, husbands average $6,000 more in annual income than do wives. A statistically significant result on this hypothesis test might lead us to conclude that the sample data do indeed support the idea that husbands average $6,000 more in income than wives.

One important caveat: Statistical significance does not necessarily imply substantive significance. That a given difference or effect is statistically significant at or beyond the conventional .05 level does not, alone, mean that the difference or effect is substantively important. Generally speaking, statistically significant results are easier to obtain as the size of the sample increases, so even fairly trivial effects can show up as statistically significant in large samples. For married men in the 2002 General Social Survey, for example, the correlation coefficient between the size of one's family of origin (that is, one's number of siblings) and one's perception of the ideal family size (the number of children one wants) was .10, suggesting that people from larger families tend to prefer having more children. Primarily because of the large sample size (N = 893), this coefficient is statistically significant (with a probability level of .002); but substantively, this is a relatively weak association (recall that a correlation coefficient of zero means no association). Even though this association is statistically significant, it may not be substantively significant.

To put this into perspective, consider that in 2002 the General Social Survey respondents who had no siblings said that they preferred to have an average of 2.79 children. Those who had one sibling preferred (on average) 2.71 children, those who had two siblings favored 2.85 children, and those with three siblings preferred 2.91 children. So although the correlation between size of family of origin and ideal family size is statistically significant, the effect is not strong—only a difference of .12 children between those who had no siblings and those who had three siblings.

Commonly Reported Tests of Statistical Significance

The Chi-Squared Test

One of the most frequently appearing tests of statistical significance is the **chi-squared** (χ^2) test. This test is often used to determine whether sample data—typically reported in a cross-classification table—are indicative of an association in the population from which the data were drawn. Chi-squared has a minimum value of 0, but its upper limit depends on the sample size and the number of rows and columns in the table. To determine its statistical significance, we can consult tables that appear in most statistics texts. For Table 11.1, the calculated chi-squared value is 225.3, with an associated probability less than .0001. This statistically significant outcome can be interpreted in at least two ways. The outcome of this test suggests that (a) the arrangement of data in the table is unlikely to have occurred by chance, and (b) an association probably exists between the independent and dependent variables in the populations from which the data were drawn. Substantively, this outcome leads us to conclude that a relationship between marital status and happiness exists—married people are happier than those who are unmarried.

Tests of Significance for Measures of Association

Most measures of association have their own specific tests of significance; but for data reported in cross-classification tables, we usually rely on the chi-squared test for information about statistical significance of the association. Generally speaking, these tests ask whether the sample data suggest that the association in the population from which the data were drawn is nonzero (that is, that no association exists). A statistically significant result suggests that the association in the population is nonzero; that is, an association probably exists between the two variables in the population from which the data were drawn.

Tests for Means

Much of the research on families and children boils down to comparisons of mean scores. For example, do children cared for in group day care centers have higher average scores on measures of aggression than children cared for at home? Do husbands of women employed full time do more housework, on average, than do husbands whose wives are not employed? Do white, African American, and Hispanic households differ in mean income?

When we are comparing means for exactly two groups—children cared for in group day care with children cared for at home, for example—we typically perform what is known as a *t*-test for independent samples, or *t*-test. The *t*-test compares the two sample means (and their variances) and produces a *t*-statistic and an associated probability value. Statistically significant *t*-statistics suggest that (a) the differences between the two groups are unlikely to be by chance, and (b) a difference in means probably exists between the two groups in the populations from which the data were drawn.

If the independent variable has more than two categories—say, ethnicity coded as white, African American, Hispanic, or other—the usual test of significance for the differences in means is known as **analysis of variance** (ANOVA). The ANOVA yields an *F*-statistic that is interpreted in much the same way as *t*: Statistically significant *F*-values suggest that that (a) the differences between the three or more means are unlikely to be by chance, and (b) a difference in means probably exists between the groups in the population from which the data were drawn.

Multiple-Regression Analysis

Multiple-regression analysis allows the researcher to assess the simultaneous effects of multiple independent variables (both categorical and continuous) on a single continuous dependent variable. For example, we might wish to study the effects of father's education, mother's age at childbirth, family income, and race on child cognitive ability. We could do a series of separate tests, examining the relationship between each independent variable and child cognitive ability separately, but the effects of the independent variables likely overlap. For example, we know that father's education and family income are positively associated: Better-educated fathers tend to have higher incomes. If we examine the separate correlations between each independent variable and child cognitive ability, we'll probably find a statistically significant relationship. How much of each correlation is shared, however? By including all the theoretically relevant independent variables in a multiple-regression model predicting child cognitive ability, we can determine how much each variable accounts for variations in child cognitive ability net of the effects of the other variable.

In such models, a regression (or slope) coefficient is reported for each independent variable in the model. In the most common form of multiple regression—unstandardized or metric regression—the regression coefficients are interpreted as the predicted amount of change in the dependent variable for a one-unit increase in the value of the independent variable. In a model predicting hours worked per week, a regression coefficient of .52 for the independent variable *years of education* indicates that the model predicts that hours worked per week increases by about .52 hours for each one-year increase in education.

A **test of statistical significance** is associated with each regression coefficient; a statistically significant result suggests that, net of the effects of all other variables in the model, the independent variable probably affects the dependent variable in the populations from which the data were drawn.

Another question that regression models can answer is how well we can predict the value of the dependent variable. The measure used here is known as the *multiple coefficient of determination,* or more commonly as R^2. R^2 ranges from 0, indicating no ability to predict the dependent variable, to +1, meaning that we can predict the value of the dependent variable perfectly without error. R^2 can also be interpreted as the proportion of variation in the dependent variable that is described by the independent variables collectively in the model. For example, a multiple regression model that yields an R^2 of .40 suggests that, taken together, the independent variables account for 40% of the variation in the dependent variable. Owing to relatively high levels of measurement error, the large number of variables that affect human behavior, and some degree of randomness in human behavior, social researchers rarely see R^2 values greater than .50.

Table 11.2 presents an example of a multiple regression table from my own research on the effects of early maternal employment on child cognitive ability. The first entry in the table—the Model R^2 of .37—indicates that the model fits the data relatively well. About 37% of the variation in the dependent variable (Peabody Picture Vocabulary Test – Revised [PPVT-R] score, a measure of cognitive ability) is accounted for by the 20 variables in the model.

The remainder of the table shows the estimated effects of each of the independent (or predictor) variables in the model. An asterisk next to a coefficient indicates that the effect is statistically significant beyond the conventional .05 level or that the sample data suggest an effect of that independent variable on the dependent variable in the population from which the sample data were drawn. For example, birth order has a statistically significant effect of –4.21 on PPVT-R score, meaning that any particular birth order (first born, second born, third born, and so on) is predicted to have a PPVT-R score 4.21 points lower than the score of the previous birth order. Low birthweight, however, does not have a statistically significant effect on PPVT-R score; that is to say,

Table 11.2   Regression Analysis Predicting PPVT-R Scores

Variable	Coefficient (b)
Model R^2	.37*
Child's characteristics:	
Birth order	−4.21*
Low birthweight	−2.00
Age (in years)	1.77*
Region of residence	
Northeast	3.92
Midwest	3.88*
South	2.42
Mother's characteristics:	
Mother's AFQT score	.15*
Age at child's birth	.08
Never married at time of child's birth	−3.55
Married at time of child's birth	1.70
Education (in years)	−.05
Currently never married	3.34
Currently married	−3.25
Family environment:	
Early family income ($1,000)	−.04
Cognitive-stimulation level	.40*
Emotional-support level	.11*
Maternal employment over first 4 years of life:	
Continuously employed full time	−4.41
Continuously employed part time	7.50
Intermittently employed	4.05
Average weekly hours employed	.35
Constant	33.43*

Sample size = 511 non-Hispanic, non-Black females.
*Indicates p < .05. Source: Based on information from Greenstein (1995).
PPVT-R is Peabody Picture Vocabulary Test – Revised;
AFQT is Armed Forces Qualifying Test.

the effect of being a low-birthweight baby is not significantly different from 0 (in other words, no effect). The key finding from this table is that none of the various measures of early maternal employment have statistically significant effects on child cognitive ability.

Some Thoughts About Statistical Analysis

Benjamin Disraeli reportedly said that that there are "liars, damned liars, and statisticians." Unfortunately, it's true that in the hands of a skilled (and perhaps unethical) researcher, statistics can be used to confirm almost any hypothesis. Perhaps more common is the uninformed or unintentional use of the wrong statistic or inappropriate technique that leads to a questionable conclusion. Nowhere is the adage "A little knowledge is dangerous" truer than in statistical analysis. Although it probably takes several courses in statistics to become really competent in this area, the material in this chapter provides a passing familiarity with the more common statistical techniques reported in the family literature.

Any good undergraduate textbook on social or behavioral statistics will provide you with additional information on the techniques discussed in this chapter. Two particularly good texts are Loether and McTavish's *Descriptive and Inferential Statistics* (1993) and Frankfort-Nachmias and Leon-Guerrero's *Social Statistics for a Diverse Society* (2000). For in-depth treatment of specific topics, consult the Sage Applied Statistics Series.

Study Questions

1. Almost every journal article about families that analyzes empirical data will report some measures of central tendency and measures of variation. Find an example of a measure of central tendency and a measure of variation in a journal article and interpret their values.

2. Find an example of a cross-classification table in a journal article on a family-related topic. What are the independent and dependent variables in the table? Briefly interpret the findings reported in the table.

3. Find an example of a measure of association in a journal article on a family-related topic. What are the independent and dependent variables in the association? Briefly interpret the value of the measure of association reported in the table. Is it statistically significant?

4. Locate an article in a family-related journal that reports the results of a multiple-regression analysis. What is the dependent variable in the analysis (that is, what variable is the regression analysis predicting)? Interpret the R^2 value for the analysis and the regression coefficient for one variable that has a statistically significant effect.

For Further Reading

DeNavas-Walt, C., Proctor, B. D., & Mills, R. J. (2004). *Income, poverty, and health insurance coverage in the United States: 2003*. Washington, DC: U.S. Government Printing Office.

Frankfort-Nachmias, C., & Leon-Guerrero, A. (2000). *Social statistics for a diverse society*. Thousand Oaks, CA: Pine Forge.

Loether, H. J., & McTavish, D. G. (1993). *Descriptive and inferential statistics: An introduction* (4th ed.). Boston: Allyn & Bacon.

12

Using Other People's Data

M any people are surprised to learn that many published studies on families and children don't use data gathered by the authors themselves; they employ **secondary data,** or data that were initially gathered by some other organization or researcher. This chapter discusses the advantages and disadvantages of secondary analysis and describes many of the most popular secondary data sets available for family researchers. Finally, it describes two sources of secondary data sets.

Advantages and Disadvantages of Secondary Analysis

Secondary data are popular for various reasons. First and foremost is cost; even a small survey can be time-consuming and expensive, and the cost of doing a limited statewide or national sample can easily run into six figures. Few researchers can afford large-scale primary data collection. Fortunately, many large-scale surveys conducted by top-notch survey organizations are available to secondary analysts at little or no charge.

A second reason that secondary analysis is popular is data quality. Nationally known survey organizations such as the National Opinion Research Center at the University of Chicago or the Survey Research Center at Temple University can afford to invest large sums of money in training interviewers and employing supervisors to handle quality-control issues. They already have interviewers in place around the country to handle personal interviews as well as computer-assisted laboratories to run telephone interviews. They have experts on staff to handle sampling issues and the design of instrumentation.

A third advantage of secondary analysis is the quantity of data. Most national surveys interview more than 1,000 respondents in a matter of weeks or even days. Few researchers could ever interview 100 respondents within a reasonable time frame. Besides the benefits for generalizability, large samples make it feasible to research groups or individuals that are uncommon in the population. For example, a national survey of 1,500 households with children would probably include several hundred single-parent households.

Secondary analysis would seem to have it all: low cost, high quality, and large quantities of data. However, secondary analysis has at least three major drawbacks. First, the data have to already exist. For example, if you want to study Asian American single-parent households, you may be out of luck: A data set may not be available with sufficient information about this particular population. Second, even if you find a study that gathered data on the appropriate population, the interview may not have included questions on the key variables needed for the analyses. Or vice versa: Even if the appropriate questions were included in the original survey, they may not have been asked of the respondents you want to study. In many surveys, not all survey questions are asked of all respondents. The well-known National Survey of Families and Households, for instance, asked extensive questions about performance of housework of all adult respondents but gathered information about child care only from parents of very young children.

Hyman (1987) presented the classic treatment of secondary analysis. Stewart (1984) addressed methods and data sources for secondary analysis. McCall and Appelbaum (1991) contrasted secondary analysis of large data sets with more traditional analyses. And Cherlin (1991) offered some general observations on the problems of secondary analysis. Brooks-Gunn, Phelps, and Elder (1991) specifically addressed secondary data analysis in developmental psychology.

If the appropriate data are available, the advantages to doing secondary analysis are tremendous. What kinds of secondary data sources are commonly used in research on families and children?

What Are Some Sources of Data About Families?

Data From the U.S. Census Bureau

Probably the best-known large-scale data sets available for research are those gathered by the U.S. Census Bureau, which conducts two series that are of particular interest to researchers interested in families and children.

The Decennial Census is conducted every 10 years. In Census 2000, about five out of six households received the *short form* questionnaire that asks about only seven topics concerning members of the household: name, sex, age, relationship, Hispanic origin, race, and whether the home is owned or rented. About one out of six households received the *long form* that asks questions about these topics plus 27 more, including education, ancestry, employment, and disability. The data from the Decennial Censuses are the closest information we have to population data about the entire United States. The 2000 Census Web site is www.census.gov/dmd/www/2khome.htm. Lavin (1994) presented a relatively nontechnical introduction to working with census data. Rives and Serow (1984) offered a more technical treatment.

For almost 60 years, the Census Bureau and the Bureau of Labor Statistics have collected information about the population of the United States with the Current Population Survey (CPS). Although the collection of labor force information each month is the primary reason for the existence of the survey, over the years, other family-related items including educational enrollment and attainment, income and poverty information, fertility, and voting activity have been added to the CPS. In January 1994, the Census Bureau began collecting data on nativity, citizenship, year of entry, and parental nativity of respondents. The universe for the CPS is the civilian noninstitutional population of the United States.

The primary goal of the CPS is the development of statistical data about the civilian labor force, but it also obtains additional information about each member of the interviewed household, as well as labor-related data for the population age 15 years or older. The monthly survey captures information about characteristics such as age, race, sex, employment status, family characteristics, and marital status. Every March, the survey includes a set of special questions, called the *annual demographic supplement.* The March supplement captures additional information such as hours and weeks worked, monetary income received in the previous calendar year, and social program use. Many of the report series used by researchers on families, children, and households come from CPS data. The CPS Web site is www.bls.census.gov/cps/cpsmain.htm.

General Social Survey

The General Social Survey (GSS) is a regular, ongoing, omnibus, personal interview survey of U.S. households conducted by the National Opinion Research Center (NORC) with Principal Investigators James A. Davis and Tom W. Smith. The first survey took place in 1972, and since then, more than 37,000 respondents have answered more than 3,500 different questions.

From Americans' racial attitudes to the number of guns owned by women to musical preferences over a lifetime, the GSS measures trends in American attitudes, experiences, practices, and concerns. The various surveys include extensive information about family-size preferences, marital history, parenting issues, abortion, and divorce.

The mission of the GSS is to make timely, high-quality, scientifically relevant data available to the social science research community. Since 1972, the GSS has conducted 24 independent cross-sectional surveys of the adult household population of the United States. These surveys have been widely distributed and extensively analyzed by social scientists around the world. To date, NORC has documented the publication of more than 4,500 articles using the GSS data.

Since 1985, the GSS has taken part in the International Social Survey Program (ISSP), a consortium of social scientists from 25 countries around the world. The ISSP asks an identical battery of questions in all countries; the

U.S. version of these questions is incorporated into the GSS. Most recently, the ISSP included a supplement on family and gender issues in 2004.

The basic purposes of the GSS are to gather data on contemporary American society to monitor and explain trends and constants in attitudes, behaviors, and attributes; examine the structure and functioning of society in general as well as the role played by relevant subgroups; compare the United States to other societies, placing American society in comparative perspective and developing cross-national models of human society; and make high-quality data easily accessible to scholars, students, policymakers, and others at minimal cost. The GSS Web site is www.norc.uchicago.edu/gss/homepage.htm.

National Longitudinal Surveys

The National Longitudinal Surveys (NLSs), sponsored and directed by the Bureau of Labor Statistics, U.S. Department of Labor, gather detailed information about the labor-market experiences and other aspects of the lives of six groups of men and women. Over the years, a variety of other government agencies—such as the National Institute of Child Health and Human Development (NICHD), the Department of Defense, the Department of Education, the Department of Justice, the National Institute on Drug Abuse, and the National School to Work Office—have funded parts of the surveys that provided data relevant to their missions. As a result, the surveys include data about a wide range of events such as schooling and career transitions, marriage and fertility, training investments, child care use, and drug and alcohol use. The depth and breadth of each survey allow for analysis of an expansive variety of topics such as the transition from school to work, job mobility, youth unemployment, educational attainment and the returns to education, welfare recipiency, the impact of training, and retirement decisions.

The first set of surveys, started in 1966, consisted of four cohorts. These four groups are referred to as the older men, mature women, young men, and young women cohorts of the NLS and are known collectively as the original cohorts. In 1979, a longitudinal study of a cohort of young men and women ages 14 to 22 years commenced. This sample of youth was called the National Longitudinal Survey of Youth 1979 (NLSY79). In 1986, the NLSY79 was expanded to include surveys of the children born to women in that cohort and called the NLSY79 Children. In 1997, the NLS program was again expanded with a new cohort of young people ages 12 to 16 years as of December 31, 1996. This new cohort is the NLSY97.

The NLSY79 respondents have been reinterviewed annually since 1979. During the years since that first interview, these young people have finished their schooling, moved out of their parents' homes, decided on continuing education and training, entered the labor market, served in the military, and married and started their own families. Data collected during the yearly surveys of the NLSY79 chronicle these changes and provide researchers with a unique opportunity to study in detail the life-course experiences of a large group of young adults representative of all American men and women born in the late 1950s and early 1960s.

The NLSY sampling design enables researchers to study the longitudinal experiences of this particular age group of young Americans as well as analyze the disparate life-course experiences of such groups as women, Hispanics, blacks, and the economically disadvantaged. The NLSY is comprised of three subsamples. The main sample is a cross-sectional sample of 6,111 youth designed to be representative of the noninstitutionalized civilian segment of young people living in the United States in 1979 and born between January 1, 1957, and December 31, 1964. Supplemental samples are designed to over-sample civilian Hispanic, black, and economically disadvantaged white youth, as well as a sample of 1,280 youth who were enlisted in the four branches of the military as of September 30, 1978.

Besides extensive information about education, training, employment, and earnings, the NLSY also contains a wealth of information of interest to researchers studying families and children. Information is also available about a respondent's marital status at each survey date, changes in marital status since last interview, and month and year that marital status was recorded, as well as information on a respondent's spouse, including birth and death dates, occupation, educational attainment, labor force status, religious affiliation, and (for select points in time) health limitations.

Fertility data include information on all pregnancies and live births, a cumulative inventory of all children reported, and the residence status of all children, contraceptive methods used, birth expectations and wantedness information, confidential abortion reports, as well as ages at menarche and first intercourse.

Types of child care used by female respondents—for example, care by relatives, nonrelatives, a day care center, nursery or preschool, self-care—types of child care payments incurred, and number of hours or days spent in child care are available for select survey years. Retrospective information about child care experiences and child care arrangements during the first three years of life for all children of at least 1 year of age were also collected.

The NLSY Children data set provides information both on the experiences of NLSY women as they became mothers and on the birth and early childhood of their children. The availability of these child data, coupled with longitudinal information on the family background, education, employment histories, and economic well-being of each NLSY mother, provides researchers a unique opportunity to examine the linkages between maternal and family behaviors and attitudes and subsequent child development. Chase-Lansdale,

Mott, Brooks-Gunn, and Phillips (1991) discussed the implications and possibilities of studying the NLSY Children for developmental psychology.

A battery of child cognitive, socioemotional, and physiological assessments has been administered biennially since 1986 to the NLSY children. Beginning in 1988, those NLSY children ages 10 years and older answered a separate set of questions that gathered information on a variety of family-, school-, and job-related topics. The NLSY has been the data source for thousands of published articles and dozens of research monographs. The NLS Web site is www.bls.gov/nls.

National Surveys of Families and Households

The National Survey of Families and Households (NSFH) includes interviews with 13,007 respondents from a national sample. The sample includes a main cross-section of 9,637 households plus an oversampling of blacks, Puerto Ricans, Mexican Americans, single-parent families, families with stepchildren, cohabiting couples, and recently married persons. One adult per household was randomly selected as the primary respondent. Wave 1 of the National Survey of Families and Households was completed in 1987. Five years later, 10,007 surviving members of the original sample were reinterviewed for Wave 2, along with many current and former spouses, partners, children, and parents. A third wave was conducted in 2001 through 2002.

A considerable amount of life-history information was collected, including the respondent's family living arrangements in childhood; the experience of leaving the parental home; marital and cohabitation experiences; and education, fertility, and employment histories. The design permits the detailed description of past and current living arrangements and other characteristics and experiences, as well as the analysis of the consequences of earlier patterns on current states, marital and parenting relationships, kin contact, and economic and psychological well-being.

This study has been undertaken explicitly to provide a data resource for the research community at large and has been designed in light of advice from many consultants and correspondents. To this end, the substantive coverage has remained broad, which permits the holistic analysis of family experience from an array of theoretical perspectives. Further information about the NSFH is available through its Web site at www.ssc.wisc.edu/nsfh/home.htm.

Panel Study of Income Dynamics

The Panel Study of Income Dynamics (PSID), initiated in 1968, is a longitudinal study of a representative sample of U.S. individuals (men, women, and children) and the family units in which they reside. It emphasizes the dynamic aspects of economic and demographic behavior; but its content is broad, including sociological and psychological measures. Because of low attrition rates and the success of recontact efforts, the sample size has grown dramatically in recent years, from about 7,000 core households in 1990 to almost 8,700 in 1995. As of 1995, the PSID had collected information about more than 50,000 individuals, spanning as many as 28 years of their lives. The study is conducted at the Survey Research Center, Institute for Social Research, University of Michigan.

Starting with a national sample of 5,000 U.S. households in 1968, the PSID has reinterviewed individuals from those households annually, whether or not they are living in the same dwelling or with the same people. Adults have been followed as they have grown older, and children have been observed as they advance through childhood and into adulthood, forming family units of their own.

Information about the original 1968 sample individuals and their current coresidents (spouses, cohabitants, children, and anyone else living with them) is collected annually. In 1990, a representative national sample of 2,000 Latino households, differentially sampled to provide adequate numbers of Puerto Rican, Mexican, and Cuban Americans, was added to the PSID database.

The PSID provides a wide variety of information about both families and their individual members, plus some information about the areas where they live. The central focus of the data is economic and demographic, with substantial detail on income sources and amounts, employment, family composition changes, and residential location. Content of a more sociological or psychological nature is also included in some waves of the study. Information gathered in the survey applies to the circumstances of the family unit as a whole (e.g., type of housing) or to particular persons in the family unit (e.g., age, earnings). Although some information is collected about all individuals in the family unit, the greatest level of detail is ascertained for the primary adults heading the family unit. Access to the PSID Web site is at www.isr.umich.edu/src/psid.

National Survey of Children

The National Survey of Children is a three-wave longitudinal study carried out by the Foundation for Child Development in 1976 and in 1981 and 1987 by Child Trends, Inc. The purpose of Wave I was to assess the physical, social, and psychological well-being of different groups of American children; to develop a profile of the ways in which children live and the care that they receive; to analyze relationships between the conditions of children's lives and measures of child development and well-being; and to replicate measures from previous studies of children and parents to permit analyses of trends over time. Wave 2 focused on the effects of marital conflict and disruption; Wave 3 examined the social, psychological, and economic well-being of the sample members as they became young adults. The base sample consists of 1,423 children. Child Trends, Inc., maintains a Web site at www.child trends.org.

Marital Instability Over the Life Course

Booth, Johnson, White, and Edwards (1991) in *Marital Instability Over the Life Course, 1980–1988* studied divorce proneness, marital problems, marital happiness, marital interaction, and marital disagreements. This study consisted of data drawn from a three-wave panel study. Five major dimensions of marital quality formed the foci of the study: divorce proneness (or marital instability), marital problems, marital happiness, marital interaction, and marital disagreements. Initially, the investigators devoted considerable attention to female labor force participation as it related to marital dissolution and divorce proneness. For the last two waves, the investigators drew heavily on a life-course perspective to guide their investigation. Life-course theories emphasize the extent to which social behaviors are a product of individuals' relative positions along a developmental continuum. A total of 2,033 cases and 1,593 variables were assessed across the three waves. Topics addressed in the study include demographics (e.g., household characteristics, race, income, religion, education); history of marriage and divorce; premarital courtship history; marital behavior (e.g., division of labor, quarreling/violence); mental and physical health of husband and wife; employment (history, status, attitudes, aspirations); attitudes about children; satisfaction about various aspects of life (e.g., marriage, home, community); problem areas in marriage, divorce, and separation (including previous discussions and current behavior, attitudes about divorce); and involvement with friends, relatives, voluntary associations, and the community.

National Survey of America's Families

The National Survey of America's Families (NSAF) is part of the Urban Institute's Assessing the New Federalism project, which tracks the effects of recent federal policy changes decentralizing many social programs. The project gathers data on economic, health, and social characteristics of children and families, to estimate well-being. Specific topics include participation in government programs, employment, earnings and income, economic hardship, educational attainment, training, family structure, housing arrangements, health insurance coverage, access to and use of health services, health status, psychological well-being, participation in religious and volunteer activities, knowledge of social services, and attitudes about work, welfare, health care, and childbearing. To date, there have been three waves (1997, 1999, 2002) of data collection on more than 40,000 U.S. households. The NSAF Web site is www.urban.org/Content/Research/NewFederalism/NSAF/Overview/NSAF Overview.htm.

The National Longitudinal Study of Adolescent Health

The National Longitudinal Study of Adolescent Health is a nationally representative study that explores the causes of health-related behaviors of adolescents in grades 7 through 12 and their outcomes in young adulthood. The project examines how social contexts (families, friends, peers, schools, neighborhoods, and communities) influence adolescents' health and risk behaviors. Data were collected in three waves between 1994 and 2002. The Web site is located at www.cpc.unc.edu/projects/addhealth.

1975 and 1985 National Family Violence Surveys

The 1975 and 1985 National Family Violence Surveys explore conflict, conflict resolution, and violence in the family. Murray A. Straus and Richard J. Gelles of the Family Research Laboratory at the University of New Hampshire conducted these surveys. Using a national probability sampling technique, interviews were conducted among households in which at least one couple resided. The survey was designed to show that physical violence between family members is more frequent than believed. There are a total of 2,143 cases and 807 variables included in the study. Topics in the study include demographics (household characteristics and composition, race, income, religion, education, etc.), history of marriage and divorce, marital behavior (conflict, violence, and resolution), employment (history, status), and satisfaction with and attitudes about various aspects of life. A similar study was conducted in 1985 to track changes in the occurrence of family violence between 1975 and 1985. The Family Research Laboratory maintains a Web site at www.unh.edu/frl.

Public Opinion Polls

Most of the major polling organizations periodically ask questions relating to children and families. Data on such topics as abortion, family values, the employment of women, and related topics are often available. The fact that some items have been repeated over long periods of time allows for interesting longitudinal comparisons. The Roper Center for Public Opinion Research at the University of Connecticut claims to be the largest library of opinion-poll data in the world; its Web site is www.ropercenter.uconn.edu. The Gallup Organization at Princeton University maintains a Web site at www.gallup .com with a searchable database of poll results.

Sources of Secondary Data Sets

For most university students and faculty, the primary source of secondary data is the Inter-university Consortium for Political and Social Research (ICPSR). Established in 1962, ICPSR is a membership-based organization providing access to the world's largest archive of computer-based research and instructional data for the social sciences. ICPSR further serves social scientists around the world by offering training facilities in basic and advanced techniques of quantitative social analysis and other resources that facilitate secondary analysis. ICPSR provides facilities and services for an international community of scholars that no one college or university could offer independently.

The data holdings cover a broad range of disciplines, including political science, sociology, demography, economics, history, education, gerontology, criminal justice, public health, foreign policy, and law. ICPSR encourages social scientists in all fields to contribute to and use ICPSR's data resources.

ICPSR includes among its members more than 325 colleges and universities in North America and several hundred additional institutions served by national members in Europe, Oceania, Asia, and Latin America. ICPSR member institutions pay annual dues that entitle their faculty, staff, and students to acquire the full range of services ICPSR provides. Individuals at nonmember schools can also order data for an access fee. Headquarters and central staff of ICPSR are located in the Institute for Social Research at the University of Michigan; the ICPSR home page is at www.icpsr.umich.edu.

Another source of large-scale data sets on children and families (as well as data on adolescent pregnancy and prevention, aging, and maternal drug abuse) is Sociometrics, a private organization that provides data sets and data extraction software. State-of-the-art research data on the American family are available through two volumes of Sociometrics' American Family Data Archive (AFDA). AFDA contains machine-readable raw data and documentation from nationally recognized studies on important issues relating to American family life, demographics, and family patterns. Data sets in the archive may be purchased individually or grouped in any number of data set combinations.

Publication as an archive enables a user to conduct variable searches across all data sets in the archive simultaneously. This capability provides the user with a means to use a single search to locate all the variables in all the data sets in the archive that match the user's search criteria. This can help the user to efficiently locate the most appropriate data set or sets from the archive for a particular research purpose. The entire archive may be particularly useful for academic departments, research centers, and agencies with multiple analysis needs that can be met in multiple ways by the collection of data sets in the archive. The purpose of AFDA is to facilitate access to the highest quality data sets on topics related to the family, family structure and change, family interaction, and family well-being. The archive comprises machine-readable data and documentation from nationally recognized studies on important issues relating to American family life, demographics, and family patterns. Sociometrics' Web page is www.sociometrics.com.

Future Trends in Secondary Data Analysis

Increasingly, major research projects are making their data available at no charge by downloading off the Internet. Often, the data, codebooks, questionnaires, and supplemental materials from a project are available. The NLSY, the National Survey of America's Families, and the NSFH are among the projects that provide data in this fashion.

Study Questions

1. Use the ICPSR Web site (www.icpsr.umich.edu) to locate a data set on a family-related topic of interest to you. Using the information contained in the abstract, answer the following questions about the project: (a) Who conducted the study? (b) When and where were the data collected? (c) What method was used to collect the data? (d) How many cases, observations, respondents, and so on are included in the data set? (e) List three general areas or topics about the data collected in the study.

2. Find three family-related articles that each use a different data set discussed in this chapter (for example, Current Population Survey, General Social Survey, National Survey of Families and Households). Briefly describe each of the articles.

For Further Reading

Booth, A., Johnson, D. R., White, L., & Edwards, J. N. (1991). *Marital instability over the life course: Methodology report and codebook for the three wave panel study*. Lincoln: University of Nebraska, Bureau of Sociological Research.

Brooks-Gunn, J., Phelps, E., & Elder, G. H. (1991). Studying lives through time: Secondary data analyses in developmental psychology. *Developmental Psychology, 27*, 899–910.

Chase-Lansdale, P. L., Mott, F. L., Brooks-Gunn, J., & Phillips, D. A. (1991). Children of the national longitudinal survey of youth: A unique research opportunity. *Developmental Psychology, 27*, 918–931.

Cherlin, A. (1991). On analyzing other people's data. *Developmental Psychology, 27*, 946–948.

Hyman, H. H. (1987). *Secondary analysis of sample surveys: With a new introduction*. Middletown, CT: Wesleyan University Press.

Lavin, T. J. (1994). *Understanding the 1990 census: A guide for marketers, planners, grant writers, and other data users*. Kenmore, NY: Epoch.

McCall, R. B., & Appelbaum, M. I. (1991). Some issues of conducting secondary analyses. *Developmental Psychology, 27*, 911–917.

Rives, N. W., & Serow, W. J. (1984). *Introduction to applied demography: Data sources and estimation techniques*. Beverly Hills, CA: Sage.

Stewart, D. W. (1984). *Secondary research: Information sources and methods*. Beverly Hills, CA: Sage.

13

Evaluating Family Programs

Many authors divide social research into two large categories. **Basic social research** is concerned with developing and testing theories about the social world, and its intended audience is scientists and academics. **Applied social research,** however, is designed to solve specific problems in society. The intended audience of applied social research is practitioners, agency workers, and government officials.

Before creating or implementing social programs or clinical interventions, it is important to gauge the need or demand for such programs. And once such programs are operating, it is reasonable to ask whether (or how well) they work. Do anger-management programs for abusive husbands reduce the rate of domestic violence? Do preschool enrichment programs enhance school performance among disadvantaged children? Do specific types of family therapy differ in their efficacy? **Evaluation research** is applied social research designed to develop, monitor, and measure the effectiveness of social programs and policies.

The methods and techniques of evaluation research are essentially the same as those used in other types of social research. Issues such as reliability, validity, and generalizability are as important as they are in studies concerned with testing or developing theories. However, there are two major complications faced by evaluation researchers. First, unlike most basic social research, evaluation research studies the needs for and effects of programs on real individuals and families. Rather than asking theoretical questions such as, "How is social class related to the likelihood of domestic violence?" evaluation researchers ask applied and focused questions such as, "How can we reduce the rate of domestic violence in XXX county?" or "Does this particular program reduce the rate of domestic violence in the YYY metropolitan area?" In other words, the activities and findings of evaluation researchers usually have meaningful consequences for the lives of individuals and their families.

A second major complication faced by evaluation researchers has to do with political concerns. Most basic social research operates in something of a vacuum, and the results of basic social research rarely get much attention outside of the journals and monographs within a particular academic discipline. Evaluation research tends to operate in a public arena, however, because most social programs (and often their evaluations) are paid for with public dollars. Publicly funded social programs will typically please some people but infuriate others. Political ideology plays a major role in the implementation, funding, and maintenance of most social programs, with those on the political left generally advocating more public spending and those on the political right usually opposing it. Evaluation researchers must be constantly aware of the conflicting demands placed on them. Agency officials often want evaluation results that indicate that their programs are working, because null results could threaten their funding. Critics of the programs typically want results that suggest that the programs don't work.

Project D.A.R.E. (Drug Abuse Resistance Education) is an excellent example of how social intervention programs can stir up controversy. D.A.R.E. is a program that uses law enforcement officers to speak in schools, promotes a zero-tolerance message, and attempts to increase peer pressure against drug use. In 1999, the D.A.R.E. program was offered in more than 80% of all U.S. school districts. Lynam and his colleagues (1999) tracked more than 1,000 students who participated in D.A.R.E. during the sixth grade. Although their research suggested some initial improvements in students' attitudes toward drug use, these changes did not persist over time. There were no changes in actual drug use initially or over a 10-year period. The authors of the study conclude that, in conjunction with the findings of many other evaluations, "the preponderance of evidence suggests that DARE has no long-term effect on drug use" (Lynam et al., 1999, p. 590).

Why, despite these and similar findings, does D.A.R.E. remain so popular with parents and school administrators? First, it is intuitively plausible that teaching children to resist the temptation to use drugs, cigarettes, and alcohol should reduce substance abuse among adolescents; consequently, the program draws a great deal of support from those who don't take the time to look at a scientific evaluation. Second, the program appears to work; most children who go through D.A.R.E. don't use drugs. What isn't so obvious to most laypersons is that, even without D.A.R.E. in operation, most adolescents don't use drugs anyway. This second point shows the necessity for rigorous evaluation of social programs and the careful use of comparison groups to determine whether a treatment program actually produces effects.

Evaluation research is directed at three major questions. First, we need to know whether a problem exists and, if so, its parameters. Is there a shortage of reasonably priced child care in XXX county? If so, what are the needs for such child care: How many children, what ages, and what rates can their families afford to pay? This first step in evaluation research is known as **needs and social impact assessment.**

Once a problem is identified, a program may be implemented to deal with it. At some point, the program's sponsors will want to know if the program is working. **Outcome research** can evaluate the results of the program to see if it is solving the problem defined during the needs assessment.

Having determined that the program is effective, **process research** asks, How does the program work? What mechanisms or processes does the program stimulate or implement that bring about the desired outcome? Each of these three steps is discussed in the following sections.

Needs and Social Impact Assessment: What Is the Problem?

Needs assessment is typically directed at one or more of four issues. First, needs assessment may be concerned with estimating the extent of a problem. If we implement a program aimed at reducing domestic violence, we first need concrete information concerning numbers of cases of domestic violence and their severity. It is important to know the scope of the problem and its distribution across such dimensions as social class, race, and geographical location.

Second, policymakers need to know something about potential use or how many individuals or families are likely to take advantage of the program. This information, combined with data on the extent of the problem, can indicate how comprehensive our intended program should be and help determine potential costs and needed resources.

Third, needs assessment might be used to prioritize problems within the communities under study. Policymakers need to know what problems the community feels are important to solve and which have the most serious implications for individuals and the community. Because financial resources are limited, the problems that require funding must be prioritized.

Finally, research might study the long-term potential for problems that might require interventions. For example, a fast-growing area might have adequate low-income health care available today, but will additional facilities be available for the growing population? Such questions require information about population growth, projected economic conditions, and the supply of and demand for health care services.

Outcome Assessment: Does It Work?

In its most basic form, outcome assessment asks simple questions: Is the program successful? Does it work? One way of operationalizing success is to ask whether the program is achieving the goals set forth in its initial formulation. A program to reduce domestic violence might aim for a 20% reduction in domestic violence cases over an 18-month period. If there is at least a 20% reduction, the program may be judged to have been successful.

Not surprisingly, there are intense political and financial pressures on agency heads to show that their programs work. About 20 years ago, a documentary film titled *Scared Straight* followed 17 male youths on a visit to Rahway State Prison in New Jersey. The fairly graphic film showed lifers haranguing teens to scare them away from a life of crime and violence. The film drew wide acclaim—it won an Oscar—and policymakers in 39 states adopted the idea for their local delinquency programs. The supporters of the *Scared Straight* program made wide-ranging claims about the success of the program at reducing delinquent behavior.

About the time that *Scared Straight* programs became popular, I served as a consultant to a local group concerned with reducing juvenile delinquency. The project used a classic experimental design—randomly assigning adolescent boys to either an experimental *Scared Straight* group that visited a local prison or a control group that did not—and followed up with multiple outcome measures over a year. The data clearly showed that there were essentially no differences between the boys in the experimental group and those in the control group in terms of arrests, disciplinary problems, truancy, or classroom performance. By all accounts, the program didn't seem to have made an impact on these boys; it certainly wasn't producing the results expected after sizable investments of public funds. However, the outcome assessment showed that there was a small (but statistically significant) difference in self-esteem scores: The boys who had made the prison visit had slightly higher self-esteem than the control group. In their pitch to the funding agency for continued support, the program director talked at great length about how the increases in self-esteem were just what the program had been aiming for all along.

The lesson here is that the goals of the program—that is, the outcomes that will indicate that the program has been successful—have to be explicitly laid out at the beginning of the program. No one involved in the *Scared Straight* program described earlier had any particular interest in self-esteem until the outcome assessment showed differences between the two groups of boys. Because the goals of the program had never been defined, almost any difference at the outcome assessment might have been presented as a successful outcome. Recently, Finckenauer, Gavin, Hovland, and Storvoll (1999) wrote about the general lack of evidence supporting the value of the *Scared Straight* program in reducing juvenile delinquency.

Process Research: How Does It Work?

Ideally, social programs aren't implemented without a strong theoretical or conceptual foundation. The theoretical foundation should describe why and how the process will work; the outcome assessment should demonstrate whether the particular implementation works or not. In the real world, however, social programs are often (some cynics would say *usually*) implemented without a theoretical basis. There is often pressure on agencies to quickly implement programs to meet some real or perceived need, or there may simply not be time in the funding cycle to conduct basic research concerning the theoretical processes underlying some behavior of interest.

Consequently, in many evaluation studies, one evaluation goal is to identify precisely how the program brings about change in its participants. If the intervention is theory driven, the instruments used to assess the process should include indicators of the variables theorized to bring about changes in the participants in the project.

The task of evaluating the process for an intervention that isn't based on an explicit theoretical or conceptual foundation is somewhat more difficult. For example, a program for battered women designed to provide them with temporary housing, clothing, food, and child care while they look for and find employment probably doesn't have a theoretical basis; instead, the program has a pragmatic basis. We don't need a theory to tell us that mothers can't look for work if they have to stay home to care for their young children. As an indication of the process involved in the program, we probably want indicators of how many job interviews the women had while in the program and to compare these data to comparable women not participating in the program. Unlike interventions with theoretical underpinnings, the decision about which variables to measure is not straightforward. In theoretically based interventions, the theory indicates which variables are important to measure; in interventions without a theoretical basis, only our common sense and professional judgment can guide us in the design of our instrumentation.

Some Thoughts About Randomization in Evaluation Research

After you've read a few evaluation studies and compared them to the discussion in Chapter 6 and other sources, you may feel like you should discount any experimental evaluation study that doesn't randomly assign respondents to treatment conditions. You may recall that a primary purpose of random assignment is to equate the treatment groups in terms of both measured and unmeasured (and perhaps unmeasurable) characteristics. Ideally, the experimental and control groups in a randomized experiment will show no pretreatment differences between factors relevant to the outcome or processes under study. After all, one of randomization's great benefits is that it eliminates all sorts of threats to validity, right?

The issue of random assignment of participants to treatment conditions in evaluation studies has been the subject of much discussion in the methodology literature. Critics of randomized experiments have made four major arguments: (1) Random assignment is not practical in evaluation research; (2) randomizing respondents to treatment conditions ignores qualitative aspects of the process under study and of the respondents; (3) such experiments give us little information when there is no statistically significant effect of the treatment on the outcome variable; and, perhaps most seriously, (4) random assignment of respondents to treatment conditions is unethical because it deprives members of the control group of efficacious treatments.

There is widespread agreement on the difficulty of achieving random assignment in evaluation studies. Random assignment is most readily achieved in studies of respondents in institutions (for example, mental patients, prisoners, military personnel, students), but these are not the kinds of situations that family researchers typically study. It is more difficult to create equivalent groups, say, of families experiencing domestic violence or of families with preschool-age children.

The second argument—that randomized experiments ignore qualitative aspects of the respondents and the process under study—is simply wrongheaded. Such experiments can study qualitative outcomes as easily as quantitative outcomes; and the fact that respondents were randomly assigned to treatment conditions does not rule out the possibility of gathering qualitative data about the respondents.

The third argument suggests that a finding of *no difference* between control and experimental groups in a program evaluation is of little value in program design and assessment. Nothing could be further from the truth. To implement a successful policy, we need to know what does and what does not work. A null finding (that is, a finding of no statistically significant difference between the experimental and control groups on the outcome variable) in a program evaluation may not tell us precisely what does work, but it certainly tells us what doesn't work. Such a finding suggests the need to find alternative theories or implementations if practitioners are to bring about change and achieve program goals.

The final criticism is perhaps the most important of the four. It holds that if the treatment is effective, it is unethical to withhold it from the members of the control group. Alternatively, if the treatment is ineffective, it is unethical to subject members of the experimental group to it, lest it raise false hopes or potentially harm the experimental respondents. Boruch (1975) responded to this criticism directly, suggesting that failure to experiment may itself be unethical, because it deprives us of the knowledge of which treatments are likely to be effective in the long run.

One way to handle the problem of withholding an effective treatment is by providing remedial treatment to the control group as appropriate. The issue of false hopes can be mitigated by careful presentation of the goals and procedures of the study to potential respondents, and the issue of potential harm to experimental respondents should be handled through a conscientious review of the procedures involved. Of course, all research should pass through the appropriate Institutional Review Board (IRB) (discussed in Chapter 14) for consideration of ethical issues and possible harm to the project's participants.

So, where does this leave us in terms of nonrandomized program evaluation studies? Although such studies are preferable to those without random assignment, we must recognize that many of the problems under study by child and family researchers don't easily lend themselves to randomized experiments. In such cases, we are limited to quasi-experimental designs (Cook & Campbell, 1979) that may leave one or more of the threats to validity discussed in Chapter 6 open to question.

The Relationship Between Applied and Basic Research

At the beginning of this chapter, I pointed out a fundamental difference between basic and applied social research: Basic social research is primarily concerned with developing and testing social theories, whereas applied social research is designed to solve specific problems in society. The two types of research are far more similar than they are different, however.

Both basic and applied research draw from the same toolkit of research strategies: surveys, experiments, nonreactive measures, observation, and qualitative techniques. Both approaches are concerned with reliability and validity of measurement. Regardless of whether we're testing a theory or developing an intervention, it is essential that our indicators provide consistent and stable measurements and that they are measuring what we think they are measuring. Both approaches have the same concerns about sampling, representativeness, and generalizability of findings, as well as technical issues such as scaling and questionnaire construction.

On another level, there is a reciprocal relationship between basic and applied social research. Applied research often draws on theories developed by basic social research to develop and implement social intervention programs. The direction of basic social research is often determined by social problems uncovered or highlighted by applied research. Workers in applied environments—social services organizations, government agencies, not-for-profit groups—must be familiar with evaluation techniques in general, but they must also be comfortable with basic research. A good general treatment of evaluation methods was presented by Rossi, Freeman, and Lipsey (1999); you may also want to look at Owen and Rogers (1999) or Berk and Rossi (1999). For a discussion about program evaluation specifically in marital and family therapy research, see Leber, St. Peters, and Markman (1996).

Study Questions

1. Locate a published example of a needs assessment, outcome assessment, or process research on a family-related topic of interest to you. Briefly describe the project and its findings.

2. Choose a family-related issue (for example, school violence, teenage sexuality, elder care) of interest to you. Describe how you might go about assessing (a) the need for programs dealing with that issue in your community and (b) the effectiveness of such programs. (How might you design an evaluation? What outcomes would you measure?)

For Further Reading

Berk, R. A., & Rossi, P. H. (1999). *Thinking about program evaluation* (2nd ed.). Thousand Oaks, CA: Sage.

Boruch, R. F. (1975). On common contentions about randomized field experiments. In R. F. Boruch & H. W. Riecken (Eds.), *Experimental tests of public policy* (pp. 108–145). Boulder, CO: Westview.

Cook, T. D., & Campbell, D. T. (1979). *Quasi-experimentation: Design & analysis issues for field settings.* Boston: Houghton Mifflin.

Finckenauer, J. O., Gavin, P. W., Hovland, H., & Storvoll, E. (1999). *Scared straight! The panacea phenomenon revisited.* Prospect Heights, IL: Waveland.

Leber, D., St. Peters, M., & Markman, H. J. (1996). Program evaluation research: Applications to marital and family therapy. In D. H. Sprenkle & M. Moon (Eds.), *Research methods in family therapy* (pp. 485–506). New York: Guilford.

Lynam, D. R., Milich, R., Zimmerman, R., Novak, S. P., Logan, T. K., Martin, C., et al. (1999). Project D.A.R.E.: No effects at 10 year follow-up. *Journal of Consulting and Child Psychology, 67,* 590–593.

Owen, J. M., & Rogers, P. J. (1999). *Program evaluation: Forms and approaches* (International ed.). Thousand Oaks, CA: Sage.

Rossi, P. H., Freeman, H. E., & Lipsey, M. W. (1999). *Evaluation: A systematic approach* (6th ed.). Thousand Oaks, CA: Sage.

14

The Ethics and Politics
of Family Research

U nlike our counterparts in the natural sciences, social scientists are faced with an ethical dilemma, a conflict between two crucial values. One is the value of scientific knowledge. The key value underlying all scientific activity is that the chief goal of science is the discovery of new knowledge (Sjoberg & Nett, 1997). The other is that social scientists recognize that (unlike their counterparts in the natural sciences) the subjects of their research are sentient beings with lives of their own. Sometimes social scientists may be forced to choose between the value of scientific knowledge and the value of the welfare of their subjects.

Ethical Issues in Research on Families and Children

Although a physicist studying subatomic particles need not worry about harming a neutron, and a microbiologist doesn't have to consider a protozoan's feelings, the rights of human research participants should be of paramount concern to social scientists. In the United States, the issue of protection of rights of human-research participants is administered by the Department of Health and Human Services (DHHS). The regulations are laid out in what is known as Title 45, *Protection of Human Subjects* (45 CFR Part 46). The National Institutes of Health's Office of Human Subjects Research has an extensive Web site listing recommendations and specific regulations at helix.nih.gov:8001/ohsr; the site even has an online computer-based training module to orient researchers to the special ethical and safety issues associated with research involving human subjects. The rights of human research subjects may be defined in four broad areas: informed consent, anonymity and confidentiality, right to knowledge of the findings, and right to remedial services.

Informed Consent

The cornerstone of ethical research on human subjects lies in the principle of **informed consent.** In general, DHHS regulations prohibit research on human subjects without the legally effective informed consent of the subject or the subject's legally authorized representative. The regulations require that each potential research participant be provided with

- A list of possible risks or discomforts
- A description of possible benefits
- A statement concerning confidentiality
- Information about who to contact concerning the study

- A statement that participation is voluntary and that the individual will suffer no adverse consequences either for declining to participate or for withdrawing at any point during the study

Anonymity and Confidentiality

By *anonymity*, I mean that no identifying information should be retained in the researcher's files following completion of data collection. *Anonymous* data are just that: There are no identifiers stored with the data, and any particular respondent in a research project cannot be directly identified. *Confidentiality*, however, has to deal with the selective release of information from the researcher's files.

Even without explicit identifiers such as names or addresses, it may be possible to identify specific participants in the study based on other reported characteristics, especially if the data include geographical information. Consequently, to minimize possible harm or embarrassment to the participants, the researcher should make every effort to conceal the identities of the participants when reporting research findings. Although DHHS regulations do not require either anonymity or confidentiality, they do require that the informed-consent agreement describe the extent to which confidentiality will be maintained.

Right to Knowledge of the Findings

The researcher has an ethical obligation to share the nature of the research findings with the research participants. In some studies, findings developed during the course of the research may affect the participants' willingness to continue in the project; DHHS regulations require that such findings be provided to the participants in a timely fashion.

Right to Remedial Services

Applied studies may study the effects of various treatments or programs designed to improve some existing disadvantage or social problem. For experimental designs in which some participants are assigned to a control condition that does not receive treatment benefits, it can be argued that the researcher has the ethical obligation to supply the beneficial treatment or program to members of the control group in a remedial fashion whenever possible.

What Is the Role of the Institutional Review Board?

At the institutional level—say, within a particular college or university—decisions concerning whether these ethical guidelines have been met for a particular research project are made by what is known as an **institutional review board** (IRB). To qualify for federal funds, all research institutions must maintain an IRB in accordance with DHHS guidelines. The IRB must consist of at least five members, one of whom is a nonscientist. At least one member must be from outside the institution. In general, all research involving human subjects must be evaluated by the IRB for compliance with the DHHS guidelines. Universities generally require that all research—whether conducted by a faculty member or student—be approved by the IRB before commencing data collection.

Certain types of research are exempt from the DHHS guidelines. In general, projects involving interviews or observations of public behavior are exempt as long as individuals cannot be identified in the data or if the data are already in the public domain.

Ultimately, the IRB has to weigh the possible benefits accruing from a proposed project against the likely or plausible risks it poses for its participants. These benefits include those of an immediate nature to the research participants as well as the importance of the knowledge that may reasonably be expected to result from the research.

Political Concerns in Research on Families

Like any other public activity, research on families and children does not take place in a vacuum. Certain theories may seem to confer privileged status on some groups or imply that other groups are somehow inferior. Research findings may be in the interest of some but pejorative to others. Those who find the results of a particular study flattering or supportive of their own ideological position will want to disseminate those results as widely as possible. Those who are unhappy with the findings of a particular study or find it to be inconsistent with their own beliefs may wish to reinterpret, discredit, or even suppress those findings.

In recent years, the debate over so-called *family values* has produced many flash points across the family-research enterprise. One area that has received much attention is the role of fathers in families. At one end of the political spectrum are neoconservatives who argue that "fatherlessness is the most harmful demographic trend of this generation" (Blankenhorn, 1995, p. 1) and that responsible fathering is most likely to occur within traditional, two-parent heterosexual marriages. At the other end of the political range are liberals and feminists who suggest that "neither fathers nor mothers are essential to child development and that responsible fathering can occur within a variety of family structures" (Silverstein & Auerbach, 1999, p. 397).

Research contributes to knowledge, and (particularly in the information age) knowledge is power. The pressures on researchers to produce findings consistent with (or at least not critical of) the existing power structure may even control employment opportunities, publication channels, and research funding.

Control of Employment Opportunities

In its most extreme form, political pressure might affect a researcher's ability to find employment. Researchers studying unpopular topics or those known for producing research findings critical of the status quo might find their job possibilities limited. One reason for the tenure system at universities is to make it possible for faculty to choose research topics without fear of dismissal on political or ideological grounds. Without such protection, faculty would constantly look over their shoulders to make sure that their work wasn't offending those in the power structure. Nevertheless, until fairly recently, research on gays and lesbians was relatively unpopular, and researchers working in this area often found their employment possibilities restricted.

Control of Publication Channels

Publication of research findings is an important part of science, because one of the fundamental norms of science is that scientific knowledge should be public and shared. Political pressures can affect the research process by limiting or suppressing publication. An interesting example of this in the child and family studies area occurred in early 1999, when the American Medical Association (AMA) fired *JAMA* editor George Lundberg for allegedly injecting the journal into presidential politics. As editor, Lundberg accepted and published a paper that was presented by the authors as a contribution to "the current public debate regarding whether oral sex constitutes having . . . sexual relations" (Sanders & Reinisch, 1999). It reported that 59% of 599 students surveyed at a large midwestern university in 1991 did not regard oral-genital contact as having "had sex." The issue was politically sensitive at the time, because the President Clinton impeachment trial was entering its second week; and a major point of contention dealt with exactly how *having sex* was to be defined.

You may recall from Chapter 3 that major professional journals publish only one or two out of every ten manuscripts submitted. Perhaps half of the rejected manuscripts either are inappropriate for publication in a particular journal—the subject matter is not within the journal's purview, for example—or are so poorly done that they do not merit serious consideration of publication. Most journal editors will freely admit, however, that they reject many competent manuscripts because of lack of publication space.

What determines which of the competent manuscripts are published and which are rejected? A study of authors of highly cited scientific papers suggested that the use of innovative methods and reinterpretations of secondary data were associated with difficulties in publishing (Campanario, 1993). In an interesting experiment, after altering the authors' names and institutions, Peters and Ceci (1980) submitted 11 articles for publication that had been previously published by mainstream journals of psychology. Only about 10% of the reviewers and editors recognized that the articles were previously published; at the same time, only about 14% of the reviewers recommended publication. Apparently, the stability of the review process over time is not high.

All of this suggests that journal editors have a great deal of latitude in deciding what does and does not get published. Inevitably, editors' personal biases affect their decisions. Some of these biases are methodological, others theoretical, and some are political. Given the large number of competent manuscripts to fill a limited amount of journal pages, all three of these biases are going to affect editorial decisions. And because faculty reappointment and tenure decisions are often based in large part on quality and quantity of publication, journal editors have a great impact on the academic job market.

Control of Research Funding

Funding agencies also have a great impact on the family research process. Agencies have to decide how much to spend and on what types of research, who will get funding to do the research, and how to make sure that the funds are used responsibly. Just as in the editorial process leading to publication, a review process leads to decisions about which projects to fund. In recent years, this funding process has become highly politicized. No better example exists than the controversy surrounding the American Teenage Survey (ATS), an $18 million project intended to survey a nationally representative sample of 20,000 adolescents. The goal of the study was "to increase understanding of the patterns of adolescent sexual and contraceptive behavior and the causes of these patterns" (Udry, 1993).

In 1989, the National Institute of Child Health and Human Development (NICHD) approved a grant proposal for this project and funded the project in May 1991. In July 1991, Secretary of Health and Human Services Louis Sullivan, appearing on a talk show on the Christian Network, was asked why he was funding this study. Sullivan had apparently never heard of ATS; but shortly afterward, he announced its cancellation. The Congressional Record (1991) reported that Senator Jesse Helms declared in the Senate,

These sex surveys have not—have not—been concerned with legitimate scientific inquiry as much as they have been concerned with a blatant attempt to sway public attitudes in order to liberalize opinions and laws regarding homosexuality, pedophilia, anal and oral sex, sex education, teenage pregnancy, and all down the line. (pp. S12861, S12862)

Fortunately for science, the ATS eventually was transformed into the well-funded and productive National Longitudinal Study of Adolescent Health.

Although criticism of the ATS came primarily from the political right, the political left can become equally involved in the scientific funding process. In 1992, the National Institutes of Health (NIH) cancelled a Genetic Factors in Crime conference that had been funded after peer review. Critics charged that the conference was inherently racist because it was to explore the genetic rather than environmental origins of criminal behavior.

The two projects described earlier were both approved by federal agencies and then, after preliminary work had commenced, had funding withdrawn. Funding agencies can also have substantial effects on the topics and methods used by researchers through their choices of projects to fund. Although nearly all granting agencies use some form of peer review, final funding decisions rest with agency personnel whose budgets are often scrutinized by members of the executive and legislative branches of government, not to mention the media. Decisions by individual researchers about what topics to study and what methodological techniques to use are undoubtedly affected by the types of studies funded in the past as well as perceptions of future funding trends.

Some Closing Thoughts

In Chapter 1, I pointed out that this text focuses on how scientific research methods can help us to understand families. One point I want to emphasize is the *conditional nature of science*. It is impossible to *prove* a theory or hypothesis because theories are not about specific locations in space, time, or culture; they are abstract and therefore universal. To prove a theory would require that its predictions be shown to hold for all empirical instances of the theory—past, present, and future. Of course, this is physically impossible. So we acknowledge the conditional nature of theory confirmation, aware that next week, or next year, or in the next century some researcher may find that the theory doesn't always apply. This is the nature of science: Theories are created, tested, confirmed, and eventually rejected and replaced. Over time, anomalies (findings that are inconsistent with the theory's predictions) are found. As the number of anomalous findings increases, confidence in the theory starts to fall, until eventually a new theory emerges that accounts for all the phenomena correctly explained by the old theory *and* the anomalies that weren't accounted for.

Science's conditional nature reminds us that perfect theories, perfect hypotheses, and perfect research designs do not exist. In particular, research designs are the result of compromises and trade-offs. In Chapter 8, I discussed the trade-off between the cost of a sample and the amount of sampling error incurred. Generally, as the sample size increases, sampling error decreases but costs increase. Consequently, the sample size drawn in most studies is a compromise between how much money is available for the project and how much sampling error the researchers are willing to tolerate. I doubt I've ever met a survey researcher who wouldn't have liked to have a larger sample than the one actually gathered. Similarly, research instrumentation often involves a trade-off. Items or questions that might have been interesting to study often have to be omitted from the research protocol because of lack of time or space. Any study published anywhere in the literature can be improved, if only in some small way: a slightly larger sample, additional questionnaire items, a better interview technique, or longer periods of observation.

As you become more experienced with reading the family research literature, I encourage you to read research reports with a critical eye. Whether you encounter them firsthand in scientific journals or monographs or second-hand in the popular press, you will probably begin to see flaws or shortcomings in the research that you read. You may read a journal article and wonder, "Why didn't they ask questions about such-and-such a topic? Why didn't they control for duration of marriage in their analysis? Couldn't they have interviewed the husbands as well as the wives in their study?" You may read a newspaper article about a new survey and have questions about the sampling procedure. Alternatively, you may see a television news story about some research findings and wonder about appropriateness of the control group in the study. As you find flaws in published research, remember that these researchers work under time and cost constraints like everyone does in every line of work.

The fact that you're asking yourself these questions is a good sign: You're becoming a critical consumer of family research. Just because an article or book is published—even in a major journal or by a well-known publisher—doesn't mean that it's the last word on the topic. Science works because we don't take our findings for granted: We are constantly questioning our methods, samples, and theories. But you can't tell the good research from the bad without some training, and that's what I hope this text has provided for you. Use your knowledge to be an active critical consumer of research to enhance your work, your life, and the lives of those around you.

Study Questions

1. Find a report of family-related research in a daily newspaper or weekly newsmagazine. What necessary information for your evaluation of the research's validity is *not* presented?

2. Find a research project using human participants in any of the major journals that publish family-related research. Evaluate the study in terms of the four major ethical concerns in this chapter. How well did the authors of the study adhere to each of these guidelines?

For Further Reading

Blankenhorn, D. (1995). *Fatherless America: Confronting our most urgent social problem.* New York: Basic Books.

Campanario, J. M. (1993). Consolation for the scientist: Sometimes it is hard to publish papers that are later highly rated. *Social Studies of Science, 23,* 342–362.

Congressional Record. (1991, September 12). Washington, DC, S12861, S12862.

Peters, D. P., & Ceci, S. J. (1980). A manuscript masquerade. *The Sciences, 20,* 16–19, 35.

Sanders, S. A., & Reinisch, J. M. (1999). Would you say you had sex if. *JAMA, 281,* 275–277.

Silverstein, L. B., & Auerbach, C. (1999). Deconstructing the essentialist father. *American Psychologist, 54,* 397–407.

Sjoberg, G., & Nett, R. (1997). *A methodology for social research: With a new introductory essay.* Prospect Heights, IL: Waveland.

Udry, J. R. (1993). The politics of sex research. *Journal of Sex Research, 30,* 103–110.

References

Amato, P. R. (1989). Who cares for children in public places—Naturalistic observation of male and female caretakers. *Journal of Marriage and the Family, 51,* 981–990.

American Psychological Association. (2002). *Publication manual of the American Psychological Association* (5th ed.). Washington, DC: American Psychological Association.

American Sociological Association. (1997). *American Sociological Association style guide* (2nd ed.). Washington, DC: American Sociological Association.

Atkinson, M. P., & Blackwelder, S. P. (1993). Fathering in the 20th-century. *Journal of Marriage and the Family, 55,* 975–986.

Babbie, E. (2004). *The practice of social research* (10th ed.). Belmont, CA: Wadsworth.

Bakeman, R., & Gottman, J. M. (1997). *Observing interaction: An introduction to sequential analysis.* New York: Cambridge University Press.

Baron, R. M., & Kenny, D. A. (1986). The moderator-mediator variable distinction in social-psychological research: Conceptual, strategic, and statistical considerations. *Journal of Personal and Social Psychology, 51,* 1173–1182.

Berk, R. A., & Rossi, P. H. (1999). *Thinking about program evaluation* (2nd ed.). Thousand Oaks, CA: Sage.

Blankenhorn, D. (1995). *Fatherless America: Confronting our most urgent social problem.* New York: Basic Books.

Booth, A., Johnson, D. R., White, L., & Edwards, J. N. (1991). *Marital instability over the life course: Methodology report and codebook for the three wave panel study.* Lincoln: University of Nebraska, Bureau of Sociological Research.

Boruch, R. F. (1975). On common contentions about randomized field experiments. In R. F. Boruch & H. W. Riecken (Eds.), *Experimental tests of public policy* (pp. 108–145). Boulder, CO: Westview.

Bridges, J. S., & Orza, A. M. (1993). Effects of maternal employment-childrearing pattern on college students' perceptions of a mother and her child. *Psychology of Women Quarterly, 17,* 103–117.

Brooks-Gunn, J., Phelps, E., & Elder, G. H. (1991). Studying lives through time: Secondary data analyses in developmental psychology. *Developmental Psychology, 27,* 899–910.

Bryant, W. K., & Zick, C. D. (1996). An examination of parent-child shared time. *Journal of Marriage and the Family, 58,* 227–237.

Buchanan, C. M., Maccoby, E. E., & Dornbusch, S. M. (1991). Caught between parents: Adolescents' experience in divorced homes. *Child Development, 62,* 1008–1029.

Bumpass, L. L., Martin, T. C., & Sweet, J. A. (1991). The impact of family background and early marital factors on marital disruption. *Journal of Family Issues, 12,* 22–42.

Campanario, J. M. (1993). Consolation for the scientist: Sometimes it is hard to publish papers that are later highly rated. *Social Studies of Science, 23,* 342–362.

Campbell, D. T., & Stanley, J. C. (1963). *Experimental and quasi-experimental designs for research.* Chicago: Rand McNally.

Carmichael, G. A. (1985). Children and divorce in New Zealand. *Journal of Marriage and the Family, 47,* 221–231.

Cauhapé, E. (1983). *Fresh starts: Men and women after divorce.* New York: Basic Books.

Chafetz, J. S. (1978). *A primer on the construction and testing of theories in sociology.* Itasca, IL: F. E. Peacock.

Chase-Lansdale, P. L., Mott, F. L., Brooks-Gunn, J., & Phillips, D. A. (1991). Children of the national longitudinal survey of youth: A unique research opportunity. *Developmental Psychology, 27,* 918–931.

Cherlin, A. (1991). On analyzing other people's data. *Developmental Psychology, 27,* 946–948.

Cherryhomes, C. H. (1992). Notes on pragmatism and scientific realism. *Educational Researcher, 14,* 13–17.

Cohen, J. (1988). *Statistical power analysis for the behavioral sciences* (2nd ed.). Hillsdale, NJ: Erlbaum.

Coltrane, S. (1996). *Family man: Fatherhood, housework, and gender equity.* New York: Oxford University Press.

Congressional Record. (1991, September 12). Washington, DC, S12861, S12862.

Cook, T. D., & Campbell, D. T. (1979). *Quasi-experimentation: Design & analysis issues for field settings.* Boston: Houghton Mifflin.

Creswell, J. W. (2003). *Research design: Qualitative, quantitative, and mixed methods approaches.* Thousand Oaks, CA: Sage.

Czaja, R., & Blair, J. (2005). *Designing surveys: A guide to decisions and procedures* (2nd ed.). Thousand Oaks, CA: Pine Forge.

Daly, K. (1992). The fit between qualitative research and characteristics of families. In J. F. Gilgun, K. Daly, & G. Handel (Eds.), *Qualitative methods in family research* (pp. 3–11). Beverly Hills, CA: Sage.

DeNavas-Walt, C., Proctor, B. D., & Mills, R. J. (2004). *Income, poverty, and health insurance coverage in the United States: 2003.* Washington, DC: U.S. Government Printing Office.

Denzin, N. K., & Lincoln, Y. S. (Eds.). (1994). *Handbook of qualitative research.* Thousand Oaks, CA: Sage.

Dillman, D. A. (2000). *Mail and Internet surveys: The tailored design method.* New York: John Wiley & Sons.

Finckenauer, J. O., Gavin, P. W., Hovland, H., & Storvoll, E. (1999). *Scared straight! The panacea phenomenon revisited.* Prospect Heights, IL: Waveland.

Fonow, M. M., & Cook, J. A. (1991). Back to the future: A look at the second wave of feminist epistemology and methodology. In M. M. Fonow & J. A. Cook (Eds.), *Beyond methodology: Feminist scholarship as lived experience* (pp. 1–15). Bloomington: Indiana University Press.

Frankfort-Nachmias, C., & Leon-Guerrero, A. (2000). *Social statistics for a diverse society.* Thousand Oaks, CA: Pine Forge.

Gelles, R. J. (1978). Methods for studying sensitive family topics. *American Journal of Orthopsychiatry, 48,* 408–424.

Gilgun, J. F. (1992). Definitions, methodologies, and methods in qualitative family research. In J. F. Gilgun, K. Daly, & G. Handel (Eds.), *Qualitative methods in family research* (pp. 22–40). Beverly Hills, CA: Sage.

Glaser, B. G., & Strauss, A. L. (1967). *The discovery of grounded theory: Strategies for qualitative research.* Chicago: Aldine.

Gomel, J. N., Tinsley, B. J., Parke, R. D., & Clark, K. M. (1998). The effects of economic hardship on family relationships among African American, Latino, and Euro-American families. *Journal of Family Issues, 19,* 436–467.

Greenstein, T. N. (1990). Marital disruption and the employment of married women. *Journal of Marriage and Family, 52,* 657–676.

Greenstein, T. N. (1996). Gender ideology and perceptions of the fairness of the division of household labor: Effects on marital quality. *Social Forces, 74,* 1029–1042.

Gubrium, J. F., & Holstein, J. A. (1990). *What is family?* Mountain View, CA: Mayfield.

Guttman, L. (1950). The basis for scalogram analysis. In L. G. S. A. Stouffer, E. A. Suchman, P. F. Lazarsfeld, S. A. Star, & J. A. Clausen (Eds.), *Measurement and prediction* (pp. 60–90). Princeton, NJ: Princeton University Press.

Hammersley, M., & Atkinson, P. (1995). *Ethnography: Principles in practice* (2nd ed.). London, New York: Routledge.

Hampe, G. D., & Ruppel, H. J. (1974). Measurement of premarital sexual permissiveness—Comparison of 2 Guttman scales. *Journal of Marriage and the Family, 36,* 451–463.

Hannan, M. T., Tuma, N. B., & Groeneveld, L. P. (1978). Income and independence effects on marital dissolution: Results from the Seattle and Denver income-maintenance experiments. *American Journal of Sociology, 84,* 611–633.

Hochschild, A. R. (1997). *The time bind: When work becomes home and home becomes work.* New York: Metropolitan.

Hyman, H. H. (1987). *Secondary analysis of sample surveys: With a new introduction.* Middletown, CT: Wesleyan University Press.

Jackson, D. J., & Borgatta, E. F. (1981). *Factor analysis and measurement in sociological research: A multi-dimensional perspective.* London: Sage.

Jacobs, J. A., & Gerson, K. (2004). *The time divide: Work, family, and gender inequality.* Cambridge, MA: Harvard University Press.

Janowitz, M. (1958). Inferences about propaganda impact from textual and documentary analysis. In W. E. Daugherty & M. Janowitz (Eds.), *A psychological warfare casebook* (pp. 732–735). Baltimore: Johns Hopkins Press.

Jones, S. (1999). *Doing Internet research*. Thousand Oaks, CA: Sage.

Kaplan, A. (1964). *The conduct of inquiry: Methodology for behavioral science*. San Francisco: Chandler.

Kneeland, H. (1929). Women's economic contributions in the home. *Annals of the American Academy, 143,* 33–40.

Krueger, R. A. (1994). *Focus groups: A practical guide for applied research* (2nd ed.). Thousand Oaks, CA: Sage.

Lannutti, P. (2005). For better or worse: Exploring the meanings of same-sex marriages within the lesbian, gay, bisexual and transgendered community. *Journal of Personal and Social Relationships, 22,* 5–18.

Larzelere, R., & Klein, D. M. (1987). Methodology. In M. B. Sussman & S. K. Steinmetz (Eds.), *Handbook of marriage and the family* (pp. 126–156). New York: Plenum.

Lavin, T. J. (1994). *Understanding the 1990 Census: A guide for marketers, planners, grant writers, and other data users*. Kenmore, NY: Epoch.

Lavrakas, P. J. (1993). *Telephone survey methods: Sampling, selection, and supervision* (2nd ed.). Newbury Park, CA: Sage.

Leber, D., St. Peters, M., & Markman, H. J. (1996). Program evaluation research: Applications to marital and family therapy. In D. H. Sprenkle & M. Moon (Eds.), *Research methods in family therapy* (pp. 485–506). New York: Guilford.

Levine, J. A., Weisell, R., Chevassus, S., Martinez, C. D., Burlingame, B., & Coward, W. A. (2001). The work burden of women. *Science, 294,* 812.

Levinger, G., & Raush, H. L. (1977). *Close relationships: Perspectives on the meaning of intimacy*. Amherst: University of Massachusetts Press.

Lewin, K. (1951). *Field theory in social science; selected theoretical papers*. D. Cartwright (Ed.). New York: Harper & Row.

Little, R. J. A., & Rubin, D. B. (1989). The analysis of social science data with missing values. *Sociological Methods and Social Research, 18,* 292–326.

Loether, H. J., & McTavish, D. G. (1993). *Descriptive and inferential statistics: An introduction* (4th ed.). Boston: Allyn & Bacon.

Lofland, J., & Lofland, L. H. (1984). *Analyzing social settings: A guide to qualitative observation and analysis*. Belmont, CA: Wadsworth.

Long, J. S. (1983). *Confirmatory factor analysis: A preface for LISREL*. Beverly Hills, CA: Sage.

Lynam, D. R., Milich, R., Zimmerman, R., Novak, S. P., Logan, T. K., Martin, C., et al. (1999). Project D.A.R.E.: No effects at 10 year follow-up. *Journal of Consulting and Child Psychology, 67,* 590–593.

Maguire, M. C. (1999). Treating the dyad as the unit of analysis: A primer on three analytic approaches. *Journal of Marriage and the Family, 61,* 213–223.

Mann, C., & Stewart, F. (2000). *Internet communication and qualitative research: A handbook for researching online*. Thousand Oaks, CA: Sage.

McCall, R. B., & Appelbaum, M. I. (1991). Some issues of conducting secondary analyses. *Developmental Psychology, 27,* 911–917.

Mead, M. (1935). *Sex and temperament in three primitive societies.* New York: W. Morrow.

Middleton, R. (1960). Fertility values in American magazine fiction: 1916–1956. *Public Opinion Quarterly, 24,* 139–143.

Miles, M. B., & Huberman, A. M. (1994). *Qualitative data analysis: An expanded sourcebook* (2nd ed.). Thousand Oaks, CA: Sage.

Minton, C., & Pasley, K. (1996). Fathers' parenting role identity and father involvement: A comparison of nondivorced and divorced, nonresident fathers. *Journal of Family Issues, 17,* 26–45.

Molotsky, I. (1999, August 31). Study links teenage substance abuse and paternal ties. *New York Times,* A16.

Morgan, D. L. (1997). *Focus groups as qualitative research* (2nd ed.). Thousand Oaks, CA: Sage.

National Telecommunications and Information Administration. (1999). *Falling through the net: Defining the digital divide.* Washington, DC: Government Printing Office.

Owen, J. M., & Rogers, P. J. (1999). *Program evaluation: Forms and approaches* (International ed.). Thousand Oaks, CA: Sage.

Pearce, L. D. (2002). Integrating survey and ethnographic methods for systematic anomalous case analysis. *Sociological Methodology, 32,* 102–132.

Peters, D. P., & Ceci, S. J. (1980). A manuscript masquerade. *The Sciences, 20,* 16–19, 35.

Peterson, R. R. (1996). A re-evaluation of the economic consequences of divorce. *American Sociological Review, 61,* 528–536.

Popper, K. R. (1964). *The poverty of historicism.* New York: Harper & Row.

Popper, K. R. (1992). *The logic of scientific discovery.* London, New York: Routledge.

Punch, K. E. (1998). *Introduction to social research: Quantitative and qualitative approaches.* London: Sage.

Reynolds, P. D. (1971). *A primer on theory construction.* Indianapolis: Bobbs-Merrill.

Richter, K. (1997). Child care choice in urban Thailand—Qualitative and quantitative evidence of the decision-making process. *Journal of Family Issues, 18,* 174–204.

Risman, B. J., & Johnson-Sumerford, D. (1998). Doing it fairly: A study of postgender marriages. *Journal of Marriage and the Family, 60,* 23–40.

Rives, N. W., & Serow, W. J. (1984). *Introduction to applied demography: Data sources and estimation techniques.* Beverly Hills, CA: Sage.

Robinson, J. P., & Godbey, G. (1999). *Time for life: The surprising ways Americans use their time* (2nd ed.). University Park: Pennsylvania State University Press.

Robinson, J. P., Shaver, P. R., & Wrightsman, L. S. (1991). *Measures of personality and social psychological attitudes.* San Diego: Academic Press.

Roethlisberger, F. J., & Dickson, W. I. (1939). *Management and the worker: An account of a research program conducted by the Western Electric Co. Hawthorne Works, Chicago.* Cambridge, MA: Harvard University Press.

Rossi, P. H., Freeman, H. E., & Lipsey, M. W. (1999). *Evaluation: A systematic approach* (6th ed.). Thousand Oaks, CA: Sage.

Sanchez, L. (1994). Gender, labor allocations, and the psychology of entitlement within the home. *Social Forces, 73,* 533–553.

Sanders, S. A., & Reinisch, J. M. (1999). Would you say you had sex if. *JAMA, 281,* 275–277.

Sayer, A. G., & Klute, M. M. (2005). Analyzing couples and families: Multilevel methods. In V. L. Bengtson, A. C. Acock, K. R. Allen, P. Dilworth-Anderson, & D. M. Klein (Eds.), *Sourcebook of family theory and research* (pp. 289–313). Thousand Oaks, CA: Sage.

Schor, J. (1991). *The overworked American: The unexpected decline of leisure.* New York: Basic Books.

Schutt, R. K. (1999). *Investigating the social world: The process and practice of research.* Thousand Oaks, CA: Pine Forge.

Secret, M., & Peck-Heath, C. (2004). Maternal labor force participation and child well-being in public assistance families. *Journal of Family Issues, 25,* 520–541.

Silverstein, L. B., & Auerbach, C. (1999). Deconstructing the essentialist father. *American Psychologist, 54,* 397–407.

Singleton, R., & Straits, B. C. (2004). *Approaches to social research* (4th ed.). New York: Oxford University Press.

Sjoberg, G., & Nett, R. (1997). *A methodology for social research: With a new introductory essay.* Prospect Heights, IL: Waveland.

Smith, T. E., Sells, S. P., & Clevenger, T. (1994). Ethnographic content analysis of couple and therapist perceptions in a reflecting team setting. *Journal of Marital and Family Therapy, 20,* 267–286.

Stack, C. B. (1974). *All our kin: Strategies for survival in a black community.* New York: Harper & Row.

Stewart, D. W. (1984). *Secondary research: Information sources and methods.* Beverly Hills, CA: Sage.

Straus, M. A., & Corbin, J. M. (1990). *Basics of qualitative research.* Newbury Park, CA: Sage.

Szinovacz, M. E. (1983). Using couple data as a methodological tool: The case of marital violence. *Journal of Marriage and the Family, 45,* 633–644.

Tashakkori, A., & Teddlie, C. (1998). *Mixed methodology: Combining qualitative and quantitative approaches.* Thousand Oaks, CA: Sage.

Thomas, W. I., & Znaniecki, F. (1918). *The Polish peasant in Europe and America.* Boston: Gorham Press.

Thomson, E., & Williams, R. (1982). Beyond wives' family sociology: A method for analyzing couple data. *Journal of Marriage and the Family, 44,* 999–1008.

Touliatos, J., Perlmutter, B. F., Strauss, M. A., & Holden, G. W. (2001). *Handbook of family measurement techniques* (2nd ed.). Thousand Oaks, CA: Sage.

Trussell, J., & Rao, K. V. (1987). Premarital cohabitation and marital stability: A reassessment of the Canadian evidence. *Journal of Marriage and the Family, 51,* 535–540.

Udry, J. R. (1993). The politics of sex research. *Journal of Sex Research, 30,* 103–110.

U.S. Bureau of the Census. (2004). *Statistical abstract of the United States* (115th ed.). Washington, DC: Bureau of the Census.

Weber, M. (1947). *The theory of social and economic organization* (M. Henderson & T. Parsons, Trans.). New York: Free Press.

Weitzman, L. J. (1985). *The divorce revolution: The unexpected social and economic consequences for women and children in America.* New York: Free Press.

White, J. M. (1987). Premarital cohabitation and marital stability in Canada. *Journal of Marriage and the Family, 49,* 641–647.

Winston, S. (1932). Birth control and the sex-ratio at birth. *American Journal of Sociology, 38,* 225–231.

Yin, R. K. (1994). *Case study research: Design and methods* (2nd ed.). Thousand Oaks, CA: Sage.

Glossary and Index

183

About the Author

Theodore N. Greenstein is a father, husband, teacher, author, and researcher, as well as Associate Professor of Sociology at North Carolina State University. He received his Ph.D. in Sociology from Washington State University and has been teaching sociology of the family, research methods, and statistics since 1976. His research program focuses on the intersection of work and family. His publications on the division of household labor, marital stability, and the effects of maternal employment on child well-being have appeared in *Social Forces, Journal of Marriage and Family, Journal of Family Issues,* and *Journal of Comparative Family Studies.* He is a member of the American Sociological Association, the Southern Sociological Society, the Council on Contemporary Families, and the National Council on Family Relations.